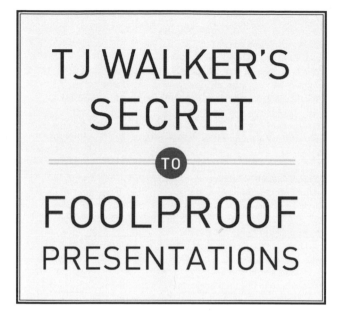

TJ WALKER'S SECRET TO FOOLPROOF PRESENTATIONS

TJ WALKER

with Jess Todtfeld

GREENLEAF
BOOK GROUP PRESS

Published by Greenleaf Book Group Press
Austin, TX
www.greenleafbookgroup.com

For ordering information or special discounts for bulk purchases, please
contact Greenleaf Book Group LLC at PO Box 91869, Austin, TX 78709,
(512) 891-6100.

Design and composition by Greenleaf Book Group LLC
Cover design by Greenleaf Book Group LLC
Cover photo by David Beyda, David Beyda Studio, NYC, www.davidbeyda.com

Publisher's Cataloging-In-Publication Data
(Prepared by The Donohue Group, Inc.)

Walker, T. J. (Timothy John), 1962–
  TJ Walker's secret to foolproof presentations : your questions answered by a
renowned speaking expert! / TJ Walker with Jess Todtfeld. -- 1st ed.
    p. : ill. ; cm.
  ISBN-13: 978-1-929774-88-3
  ISBN-10: 1-929774-88-5
1. Business presentations. 2. Public speaking. 3. Interpersonal communication. I.
Todtfeld, Jess. II. Title. III. Title: Secret to foolproof presentations
HF5718.22 W25 2009
658. 4/52   2008941990

Part of the Tree Neutral™ program that offsets the number of trees
consumed in printing this book by taking proactive steps such as
planting trees in direct proportion to the number of trees used.
www.treeneutral.com

TreeNeutral™

Printed in the United States of America on acid-free paper
09 10 11 12 13   10 9 8 7 6 5 4 3 2 1
First Edition

Contents

USING POWERPOINT AND VISUALS

DELIVERING YOUR PRESENTATION

TROUBLESHOOTING AND ADAPTING

DEVELOPING A LIFETIME PRESENTATION IMPROVEMENT PLAN

Introduction

During the last quarter of a century I have coached tens of thousands of people—sales executives, CEOs, civic leaders, prime ministers, members of the U.S. Congress and British Parliament, athletes, entertainers, pageant winners, and ordinary business-people—on how to be better presenters. And through all of those sessions and speeches, I have found that there really is one big secret to giving a foolproof presentation. Would you like to know what it is?

The Secret

Develop an audience-focused perspective rather than a speaker-focused perspective.

You might think that you don't deliver presentations to audiences because you talk to only a couple of people at a time. But anytime you speak to convey information or persuade people toward a course of action, you are presenting to an "audience." Simply put, an audience is anyone you present to, whether that is one single person listening to your sales pitch for a new phone service, twenty people listening to your department update at a weekly staff meeting, or two thousand people listening to your keynote address at an annual trade convention.

So, regardless of setting, I absolutely believe—because I've seen it time and again—that the reason most present-ers fall flat is because they are focused on what *they* want to say and how *they* want to say it. Presenters rarely stop to consider what the audience wants to hear or how the audience wants the message delivered.

Other business authors and leaders talk about the "wisdom of the crowd" when trying to make important market decisions: that is, a mass of consumers will always have a better idea of what will be well received in the market than a handful of elite executives. For me, this idea logically filters down to the presenter and her audi-ence. The audience you speak to is never wrong, in the same way that if you launch a new product and it fails in the marketplace, consumers were not wrong for refusing to buy it. The presenter should place faith in the wisdom of the audience—the audience will be a much better judge of what will be well received in a presentation. They are the ones who have to receive it, right?

As an example, let's look at some common concerns most presenters have:

What does my audience want to hear?
Have you asked your audience?
What stories work best?
Have you asked your audience?
Do my slides work?
Have you asked your audience?
Am I overwhelming my audience?
Have you asked your audience?

All of these questions, and almost any others you can come up with, can be easily answered—for free—just by asking your audience.

Now, I'm not trying to convince you to put this book down. I'm trying to explain how *valuable* it is. Instead of spending a lot of time and effort polling hundreds or thousands of audience members and trying to get honest feedback, you can read this short book (in which I will also tell you how to effectively poll your audience members and get honest feedback). In a succinct and compact read, I am offering you the answers your audience will almost certainly give you. But why do you need to read it?

Why are presenting skills so important?

Because nothing big in life ever happens just by sending a memo or an e-mail. The biggest moments in your life are about presentations. A job interview, a new business pitch, a marriage proposal, a request for funding, an interview on live network TV news, and a request for a promotion—these are all presentations of one kind or another. When a topic is important, human beings want to hear from you—directly. Presenting is not the best way to transfer a large body of facts to people, but it is the best way to make people sit up and take notice, to make them understand that you think something is extremely important, and to convince them that they should think it is important too. Presenting is a way of putting a spotlight on an idea that no other medium can ever match—not e-mail, not memos, not even TV or radio.

Presentation skills are the only universal factor among wildly successful people in every field, yet they are rarely taught in business schools and other institutions of higher learning. Every big corporation in the world is packed with mid-level managers, many of whom may have done better in school and have higher IQs than their bosses. But these mid-level managers often develop reputations for being behind-the-scenes players. Why? Because they either avoided or failed at opportunities to speak out. They didn't raise their hand in meetings. They turned down the opportunity to fill in for the boss on a critical client presentation. They developed a reputation for hard work, but also as "not the sort of person we can put out front, who can effectively represent our company to the industry and to the rest of the world." This is a tragedy of human potential, but it is one that can be fixed at any age, by anyone.

I believe that any human being who has ever had even one interesting conversation with one other person already has all of the skills needed to be a great presenter—all you need to do is figure out how you met the needs of your audience (the other person in the conversation) and transfer those strengths into your presentation. This book will take this one guiding principle and show you how it applies to the most common questions you likely ask yourself before giving any speech. By focusing on the needs of your audience—of one or one thousand— and following the advice in this book, you will deliver foolproof presentations—every time.

PREPARING FOR YOUR PRESENTATION

How can I get over stage fright or nervousness?

I'd like to be able to tell you something comforting—
"It's going to be fine!" or "You'll do great if you just
believe in yourself!" I wish I could tell you to just chat
positive affirmations or picture your audience naked or
visualize a standing ovation. The problem is that none of
those things will prevent you from giving a lousy presentation, so they shouldn't help ease your anxiety either.

The reality is that you have good reason to be nervous. You are probably nervous because at some point
in your life, you've given a lousy presentation. And I'm
sure you've attended a lot of lousy presentations. So, you
know that chances are you're going to bomb. Okay, okay,
that may have been a little harsh. But I didn't say it to
be mean-spirited or to ruin your confidence. The fact is
that most speakers bore their audiences. Most presenters

VISUALIZING YOUR AUDIENCE WITHOUT ANY CLOTHING ON MIGHT ACTUALLY MAKE YOU *MORE* NERVOUS.

give unmemorable data dumps. Most speakers communicate absolutely nothing (and by communicate, I mean give the audience something to remember). So, at the risk of freaking you out, I really think that you and most presenters should be MORE nervous, not less nervous, when you speak.

But I also recognize that being excessively nervous can really ruin your shot at giving a great presentation. I'm going to help you deal with it on a deeper level and in an audience-oriented way. In fact, that's what this book is designed to do. What, then, is the secret to getting over your fear of public speaking?

The Secret
Preparation, preparation, preparation—always with your audience in mind.

- First, create an interesting presentation designed to give your audience what they want and need.
- Second, understand what your audience is seeing by recording yourself giving the presentation, watching the recording, adjusting your delivery or content, and then recording the presentation again.
- Third, get feedback from real people by giving the presentation to a few willing colleagues and asking them specific questions about your content and delivery.
- Fourth, prepare for your specific audience by asking them questions before you start.
- Fifth, prepare for your next presentation by asking your audience how you did.

I'll explain how to do all of these things throughout the rest of this book. If you follow my advice, you'll have a lot more confidence in what you are saying and doing, and your presentations will improve dramatically. It's not that hard, yet very few people ever take the time to prepare fully and properly.

While I do want you to take every speaking opportunity very seriously—and prepare accordingly—I don't want you to feel fear. I want you to look at every presentation as a chance to learn and have fun, and the surest way to make that happen is to feel secure in your readiness.

TJ TV: Want more advice about overcoming your nerves? Go to www.tjwalker.com, register if you're a first-time visitor, and then enter the words OVERCOMING NERVES in the TJ TV form.

How can I avoid making a bad impression?

I n every presentation, there are three possible outcomes for the presenter:

> A good impression was made.
> A bad impression was made.
> No impression was made.

The biggest blunder most presenters make is not that they humiliate themselves or freeze up on stage. The huge mistake most presenters make is that they show up, give their presentations, and come across as professional, polished speakers. They give their presentations exactly as planned. No snags. Then they sit down.

So, what's the problem? Ask the audience members what any one of these speakers said and they say, "Great presentation! Very professional." The audience doesn't remember anything the presenter actually tried to communicate! The presenter had an opportunity to communicate a message, but he blew it by being guilty of sameness. In an effort to avoid making a bad impression, the presenter ended up making no impression at all.

Think of how many presentations you hear at the office, civic clubs, sales meetings, trade conventions, church, or school. And yet, how many do you remember six months later, six days later, or even six hours later? Foolproof speakers realize this problem, so they don't waste their time trying to avoid bombing.

The Secret
Don't focus on not making a bad impression. Spend your time figuring out how to leave a *lasting* positive impression.

The solution is to give real thought to becoming more memorable, not to convey more facts and data. This doesn't necessarily mean more time, expense, or fancy props; it just means being a little more creative and setting yourself apart from the crowd of average presenters. When Steve Jobs wants to demonstrate how thin his new laptop is, he doesn't just flash up a slide that says "Laptop thickness: 0.25 inches." That would be boring.

Instead, he demonstrates how thin the laptop is by pulling it out of an envelope. Total cost: 79 cents. The image is so powerful that it can't be forgotten days, weeks, or even months later.

What are you doing to make sure you leave an impression—any positive impression—on your audience? When you consider this question, you'll realize that it's not really a gamble to try that new story or a PowerPoint slide with edgy humor. Or to ask audience members questions even though you don't know how they'll respond. All of these attempts to mix it up will increase the odds that you don't end up instantly forgotten. Doing what everyone else is doing—playing it safe—just to avoid bombing is the real gamble, because you will likely make no impression on your audience at all.

You must do something, anything, in order to get people to leave your presentation with a positive impression of you and your ideas.

TJ TV: Want to know how Warren Buffett gets people to remember what he says? Go to www.tjwalker.com, register if you're a first-time visitor, and enter the words REMEMBER BUFFETT in the TJ TV form.

Should I rehearse,
and for how long?

Yes, you should rehearse. Yes, yes, yes, yes, yes. From a presentation coach's perspective, the following sentence is the dumbest in the English language:

"I don't want to rehearse because I don't want to seem canned; I want to seem spontaneous and fresh, so I had better wing it."

Ugh!

It is true that if you try to memorize your speech or deliver your presentation in the exact same way every time, you will set yourself up for failure (exceptions for any reader who is a trained Broadway actor). But rehearsing your speech should never be about memorizing words or movements.

If you don't rehearse, you are throwing the rough draft of your presentation at your audience. And rough drafts are, well, rough. Here is a question I ask every one of my clients: "How often would you dictate a letter to an assistant, and then instruct your assistant to send it to all of your clients, your boss, and the media without editing it, spell-checking it, putting it on a nice letterhead, or getting another set of eyes to review it?"

Clients usually chuckle and say, "Never," and I imagine that is what you would say too. But that's exactly what you are doing if you give a presentation without first rehearsing it. Most people are nervous before they give a presentation, yet they're calm when they send out a letter to clients and prospects. What's the difference? With a letter you have the opportunity to work through several drafts and get to a point of confidence that it is the best it can be and is devoid of major errors before you send it out. That's why you aren't nervous about sending letters.

The real reason that you—and most people—fear public speaking is that you fear the unknown. You don't know if your content is interesting, you don't know if you look or sound stupid, and you just don't know what the audience thinks about you or what you're saying. When you think about it, this makes perfect sense.

Let's take another example from our everyday lives. If someone forced you to get dressed in the morning in the dark and didn't let you look in the mirror once before leaving your home, would you be nervous about your appearance? Of course you would. You'd be worried that you missed shaving half of your face or that you put lipstick on crooked. I'm sure that you look in the mirror many times before leaving in the morning. But it's not as if you have to look at your own face all day long. You look in mirrors because you want an accurate sense of how the rest of the world sees you. We all have an "editing" system for putting on our public face and clothes. The result? When you show up at the office or in front of clients, you probably aren't worried about your face or your hair or your clothing. You might not think you're perfect (I hope you don't), but at least you are confident that you have put your best face forward.

The same principle that applies to writing a letter or getting ready to leave your house in the morning can apply to presenting. There is no good reason not to go through drafts of your presentation until you really like it and feel totally comfortable with it. And I'm not talking about rewriting the words of your speech or reading it over and over again to yourself. A presentation is NOT the words you've created on paper or on a computer screen. A presentation is you actually speaking. So, how do you rehearse?

The Secret
You must record your entire presentation on video and then watch it.

You absolutely must do this. It is the only way to find out whether your presentation is any good. You have to watch yourself giving your speech. You can't just stare at words written on paper. The presentation is you actually speaking, so you have to edit the rough draft of you actually speaking.

Over and over again, clients ask, "TJ, do I really have to watch myself? I hate watching myself on video!" Sorry, but you do. The same way you have to read a letter before you send it or look at yourself in the mirror at least once before you leave for work in the morning. Is it painful to watch yourself? Yes. But this is less painful than wasting the time of people you are speaking to because you were boring or hard to follow. So grab a video camera, a cell phone with video capture, a Webcam, or any other video device and record your speech. Then watch it.

This brings up a point that never ceases to amuse me. Countless how-to books on speaking and presenting use phrases like, "If a video camera is available, try to record your speech . . ."

If a video camera is available? What year are we in, 1910?

You don't see books on resume writing that say, "If a computer is available and if you can find a spell-check program, you may wish to check the spelling in your resume before sending it out." It is equally absurd in this day and age not to use a video recorder as you rehearse your presentation. For starters, your cell phone

THE LACK OF A REAL AUDIENCE IS NO EXCUSE NOT TO
REHEARSE YOUR PRESENTATION.

probably captures video and your computer likely has a
Webcam that will capture your rehearsal, not to mention
any digital still camera. Personally, I never go anywhere
without a Flip Digital video recorder; it's no larger than a
cell phone, has one button, costs less than dinner for one
in Manhattan, and plays back instantly.

And don't try talking to a mirror. It's a complete waste
of time. It will take you a half hour to get past the first

line. And instead of focusing on delivering ideas to an audience, you will focus on your big nose or some part of your face you don't like. Plus, there will be nothing to analyze once you are done.

The video creates something tangible that allows you to critique your strengths and weaknesses. That's important when learning most new skills. Imagine if, when you were in elementary school, you tried to learn how to write essays by dictating one to your English teacher and never reading the transcript. Now, imagine that when she graded your essay your teacher didn't show you the words. Instead she just told you what you did well or poorly. Do you think you ever would have become a competent writer that way? Of course not.

You have to see video of yourself speaking if you want to improve, and there is absolutely no excuse not to do so.

I will warn you, if you have never seen a video of yourself speaking, you will not likely enjoy watching one. Tough! Your audience has to watch you; shouldn't you know what they are seeing and hearing?

If you are like most people, here is the response you'll have after watching yourself: "Ugh, I hate my speech! I am so deadly dull it's not funny. I never imagined I would sound so boring and monotonous. I would fall asleep if I had to watch this speech." Well, at least now you know how your audience will feel. The good news is that you still have time to fix this disaster of a speech. When I ask clients what they want to do to improve their presentations, the first response is usually, "Throw the whole thing in the trash can!" And sometimes that may be the best thing.

Practice alone is not enough—especially if you are practicing a long, boring, abstract presentation. I can't tell you what to say, but I can tell you that if you hate your speech, there is an excellent chance your audience will too. So, come up with a new one. The key is to get rid of the bad, boring, abstract content from your speech and replace it with interesting examples, case studies, and success stories. (More about this later in the book.) But here's the rub: The best way to get rid of stuff you don't like is to focus on the parts of your presentation that you *do* like so you can do more of it.

Now, for the second part of the question—how long should you rehearse? You can't just try this once and move on. You have to rehearse, record, and review your presentation again. Are you happy with your presentation? If not, keep revising, rehearsing, recording, and reviewing until you are happy. Is this tedious? Sure. But you already do this with printed documents going out of your office. Why is your presentation less important than a printed document? Keep refining your speech and keep watching it until you reach a magical moment: when you can watch your own speech and actually love what you see, when you can watch the video and say, "Wow, that's a great presenter. If I can do half as well in real life, I will be the best presenter there." This might take you five hours or it might take you five days. Either way, your audience doesn't care. They just want your best.

Here's the payoff: When you are watching a video of yourself and you can clearly see that you look comfortable and confident and that you are expressing your ideas in an interesting and memorable way, a funny thing happens—you become a better presenter. That first feeling of confidence goes a long way.

Please, please, please, I beg of you: Record your presentation rehearsal and keep rehearsing until you love what you see. If you disregard everything else in this book but follow this one piece of advice, you will have unlocked most of the secret to giving foolproof presentations, because you'll actually get a chance to see yourself the way your audience sees you!

TJ TV: Want some extra strategies on maximizing your rehearsal time? Go to www. tjwalker.com, register if you're a first-time visitor, and enter the words REHEARSAL TIME in the TJ TV form.

How can I find out whether my presentation is effective?

I am constantly amazed at how many hard-nosed executives who want to quantify everything they do—from evidence on what is the cheapest paper clip to clearly defined goals for every step they take—suddenly go all squishy when it comes to giving presentations. Instead of focusing on how to specifically communicate what they want the audience to remember and testing the results, they try to just get through it and cover all the bases. They see the ability to deliver a good presentation as a "soft" skill. But there is absolutely nothing soft about delivering effective presentations. It is a highly quantifiable endeavor.

So, when a client says something foolish to me like, "I guess I'll never know for sure whether what I'm saying is sticking with the audience," I get a little peeved. Of course there is a way! How?

The Secret

You have to test your presentation in front of a real, live audience and then ask them what they remembered.

Videotaping your presentation is a spectacular way to make sure you're saying what you want to say in a clear and interesting manner. But you'll never know whether what you're saying is memorable to the masses (of one or one thousand) if you don't test it with an audience—repeatedly.

The beauty of a presentation is that it is much easier to test than, say, a new drug, which might take ten years, or new software, which might take ten months. Testing a presentation takes just about as long as you need to deliver it and then ask some questions.

The goal of every presentation is to make the audience remember what you wanted to communicate. If you want to know whether your presentation works, all you have to do is ask people who listened to you what they remember. Very simple. If they remember what you wanted them to, your presentation worked. If they don't remember what you wanted them to, your presentation didn't work. And if your audience doesn't remember your message, it's not their problem—it's yours.

Let's start with the first test. Let's say you have to give a sales presentation to twenty important prospects this Thursday afternoon. Simply round up four colleagues and ask them to watch your presentation Tuesday at lunchtime. When you are done with your presentation, ask your colleagues two specific questions:

1. Can you tell me every specific message point from my presentation that you remember?
2. Can you tell me every PowerPoint slide you remember? (Obviously, this question is necessary if you are using slides. If you are using some other form of support, you can adapt this question, such as, "Which video or audio clips did you remember?" or, "Which whiteboard drawings did you remember?")

Write down their answers. Any message that was important to you that was not instantly thrown back in your face means you have a problem. You now have empirical evidence that the way you are communicating your most important messages is not working. Go back to the drawing board and start over.

Any slide or other element you used for support that your sample audience didn't remember should be cut or revised. If they didn't remember it, you have empirical evidence that the way you graphically or otherwise supported your idea isn't working. Take anything from your presentation that your test group didn't remember and throw it in the trash—it is worthless! Maybe it just isn't necessary, or maybe it needs to be replaced with something better.

The secret to knowing whether your presentation works really is this simple, and yet it is a challenge, because it means breaking old, ingrained habits. It means preparing and giving speeches based not on what is easy or convenient for us as presenters but, instead, on what is easy and convenient for audience members to understand and remember.

The next step in the testing process is to ask your actual audience the same questions you asked your sample group after you've delivered your presentation. This is particularly important if you have to deliver the same or similar presentations over and over. Again, I am amazed at how many bottom-line-focused businesspeople throw away billions of dollars' worth of market research that they could be gathering free of charge—just because they don't think to ask their audiences a few simple questions.

After every presentation you give, ask one or more of the people you spoke to for feedback on what they remember. In addition to the two questions I already gave you, try these:

- What stories, case studies, problems, and numbers do you remember?
- If one of your colleagues missed the presentation, how would you describe it to her in a couple of minutes or less?

Your audience will give you great, specific feedback if you ask specific questions like these. Do not ever ask audience members, "How'd I do?" They will say, "You did great!" And that is worthless feedback. Also beware of responses like, "Wow! The presenter was excellent. He seemed so poised. He was interesting and funny. I liked the presentation a lot." If that's what you hear, it means you communicated nothing. Sure, we want people to form nice impressions about us as speakers, but our primary goal is to communicate messages. If all the audience remembers is what they thought of our speaking style, then we failed.

If you want to test your presentation in an even more thorough manner, wait three days and then e-mail people in the audience and ask them what ideas and messages from your presentation they found to be most useful. If you really communicated effectively, you'll get responses of substance and insight. If you failed to communicate, you'll get e-mails like this one: "Hi, Jim. Great speech! See you soon, Brandy."

You can complain that there is no time to test your presentation in advance because you are busy rewriting your speech or redoing your slides until 2:00 AM the morning of the presentation. (This is a horrible thing to do, by the way, but that still doesn't get you off the hook. In this case, you just have to use the presentation itself as the test and make sure you ask your audience members specific feedback questions.)

When you get specific feedback from your audience, you can refine, tweak, and improve your product—in this case your presentation—much in the same way cars and expensive household appliances—even ordinary household products—are improved by using feedback from expensive focus group testing. But your focus group research is completely free! Take advantage of it.

In most larger organizations, this type of feedback is rarely gathered or incorporated into major presentations. I always get a kick out of people who speak about Six Sigma strategies for seeking out defects and improvements in business practices, yet never seem to think that presentations should be a part of this process. This is a real bureaucratic danger: A marketing or sales presentation is written and rewritten twenty times, and then seventeen different people review and approve it before it is ever tested in front of an audience. And then the presentation is treated as if it were the Gospel and to change one word of it would be a sacrilege. It's the same boring presentation, therefore, that's given thirty times over the next eleven months. This is such a gigantic waste of money. It's fine for corporations to approve key messages at an executive level, but the delivery of those messages should be continually improved and refined. No presentation is perfect. Every presentation could be improved. If you ever have to convey the same set of messages to different audiences, each presentation should be better than the last one.

Consistently giving great presentations has nothing to do with the mood of the audience, the person who spoke just before you, or luck. Like any world-class businessperson knows, you make your own luck. You can foolproof your presentations by testing before and after every one. It really doesn't take much time, and the results will be well worth it.

TJ TV: Want another example of how to improve your speech? Go to www.tjwalker.com, register if you're a first-time visitor, and enter the words FRANKLIN IMPROVE in the TJ TV form.

What are the realistic big picture goals I should shoot for in every presentation?

I think you should have five specific goals every time you present.

First, you should want to look comfortable, confident, relaxed, and authoritative. You want to look your best. Partly because we are all vain, but mostly because it will generally make us seem more credible and therefore will make our messages more memorable and believable. By looking comfortable and relaxed, we allow our audience to focus on our message without distractions.

Second, you should want to be understood. If you use too much jargon or insider lingo, no one will understand you. If you speak too quickly or too softly, no one will understand you. If you use language that is too high-level or low-level for your audience, no one will understand you. And if people don't understand you, then no real communication is going to occur.

Third, you should want people to remember your messages. This is a big one. This is where presenting gets tricky. Lots of people can speak in ways that are understandable, but few people can speak in ways that are memorable. Most people present in a manner that is so abstract and fuzzy that although they may be understood, nothing sticks in the memory of the average audience member. This is a critical problem if left unsolved. If you present information and no one remembers anything you said, what have you accomplished? Absolutely nothing.

There is only one type of presenter I know of where it doesn't matter whether the audience remembers anything—the standup comic. If I go to a comedy show on Saturday night and have a lot of laughs with friends, but I don't remember any of the jokes Sunday morning, that's okay. I still had a fun Saturday night. But if you are giving a business presentation and nobody remembers anything you said, it was a failed presentation.

Fourth, you should want the people you are presenting to to take some action, in the form of placing an order, voting for you, hiring you, authorizing your project, or at least changing some small thing about the way they work. Unless you are a philosophy professor and you are speaking just for the intellectual enrichment of your audience, when you present to people, you typically are doing so because you want them to take a very specific action.

Fifth, you should want people who heard you present to tell other people what your message is. You want people who didn't write down anything you said to be able to tell their colleagues, associates, friends, and business partners what they learned from you. This way, your presentation continues to benefit you and others—it lives on.

The Secret

To be a successful presenter, focus on confidently and authoritatively delivering a presentation that your audience understands and remembers, and that will drive listeners to take action and tell others about your message.

Remember, it's not communication if it simply comes out of your mouth. It is only an act of communication if it comes out of your mouth and is received, processed, and understood by someone else. And it is only effective communication if you get that person to act on your messages. The foolproof presenter realizes that it is possible to accomplish all five of these goals each and every time you speak. Every single presentation is an opportunity both to make a connection and to communicate with your audience.

TJ TV: Want to see an example of John F. Kennedy defining his goals? Go to www.tjwalker.com, register if you're a first-time visitor, and enter the words BIG PICTURE in the TJ TV form.

CREATING YOUR PRESENTATION

What is the best way for me to start my presentation?

Unfortunately, I cannot offer a specific answer to this question that will meet everybody's needs. Because there is no one, perfect way to start a presentation, I'm going to tell you what you shouldn't do and then give you the secret of a good beginning.

You shouldn't start your presentation or speech the way most presenters do. Why? Because most presenters start by talking about themselves. This is a critical moment in the presentation, and as a presenter, you have to make a fundamental choice: Are you going to focus on yourself or on your audience? If you focus on your audience, you will likely be a success. If you focus on yourself, no matter how polished you are, you will likely fail.

What follows is a lesson in what *not* to do.

"Good morning. My name is TJ Walker." (The audience already knows this because I was just introduced or my name is on the agenda.)

"I am the CEO of Media Training Worldwide." (Again, the audience already knows this because that's how I was introduced or it's on the agenda.)

"I am very happy to be here today." (The audience doesn't care about my happiness at this stage of the relationship.)

"Before I begin (actually, I have already begun), I'd like to tell you about the history of my company. Back in 1984 . . ." (Why does anyone want to hear my life story at this point?)

The problem with this approach is that everything the presenter is saying is about himself and is boring, a cliché, or irrelevant to the audience. He might eventually get to some interesting content, but by then there is the real danger that half the audience has zoned out.

It doesn't have to be that way.

Deep down I am an optimist, and I believe that most people are good-spirited. But I don't believe that audiences are terribly interested in the well-being of the presenter. It's not that the people we speak to wish us ill will, it's just that they are focused on themselves, their lives, and their careers. So, the quicker we talk about *them*, the better off we are. What, then, is the best way to start a presentation?

The Secret
Talk about the audience's needs or desires right off the bat.

Here is an example of how I start a presentation when I am working with a small group of executives in a session on presentation training.

> So, why are we here? Jim, you mentioned that you are comfortable when you are sitting down presenting to a small group, but you get uncomfortable when you have to stand and talk to more than twenty people. We'll work on ways to overcome that.
>
> Sally, you mentioned that you don't mind talking to a room full of strangers, but you get really nervous talking in your weekly staff meetings. We'll come up with tips on how to get comfortable there.
>
> Sandy, you feel like your PowerPoints are dragging you down. We'll learn some new ways to make Power-Point add to your presentation.

Now, you might be thinking that I haven't said anything particularly eloquent or brilliant—or even that interesting. But I can assure you that Jim and Sally and Sandy find this opening incredibly interesting because it is all about them. They are riveted to the presentation because it is personal, and I've told them exactly what I'm going to do FOR THEM.

How did I get all of this inside information about the people I am speaking to? Did I do Google searches? Interview their assistants? Spend four hours reading their profiles on the company Web site? No. All I did was have a thirty-second conversation with each of them ten minutes before my presentation. I talked to them about their needs, listened to their concerns, and personalized the start. It's simple and effective.

The biggest hurdle most people face with this approach is that their speeches are written out in advance, including the beginning. They feel that if they don't have a start already prepared, they'll fumble and falter and fail. It's also difficult to know how to personalize your presentation if a speechwriter or corporate communications person created your speech for you. Speechwriters may prepare a beginning that is overly formal. Marketing experts may want you to start by listing your top five corporate messages. These are all mistakes.

The technique I used works well with a small group of people or even just one person. But it also works well with an audience of one hundred. Obviously, you can't talk to one hundred people before you start or reference what they all might say. But if you reference what four or five people in the room said, it will make the audience relate to you better and feel like you are giving them content that is fresh and relevant. It gives your presentation an un-canned quality, and they will appreciate it.

Even when you personalize your approach, there is no one ideal way to start a speech. It could be with a question, or it could be with a funny story. But it doesn't have to be witty or clever as long as it is interesting and relevant to your audience.

In my experience, audiences truly reward presenters who concentrate on the audience right from the beginning. And they will reward you with what really counts—their attention, their focus, and their positive memory of what you said.

TJ TV: Avoid the mistakes this presenter makes during his opening remarks. Go to www. tjwalker.com, register if you're a first-time visitor, and enter the words OPENING REMARKS in the TJ TV form.

How long should my presentation be, and how can I be more concise?

According to a U.S. Department of Defense study conducted in 1974, the perfect length of a presentation is 17.4 minutes. Really. This is what the research found.

Don't you believe it.

Here is the only rule you need to follow when it comes to presentation length:

The Secret

Speak for as long as you need to, provided that you are consistently interesting and memorable to the people in front of you.

I have personally seen Anthony Robbins hold the attention of a room filled with five thousand people from 10:00 AM until midnight. And the crowd wanted more! And I'm sure you've seen lots of speakers who put everyone to sleep in two minutes. So, a twelve-hour speech can seem too short if you are incredibly interesting, and a three-minute speech can be too long if you are dreadfully dull.

Many speakers make the mistake of conceptualizing their speech in terms of length. They think, *I am giving a thirty-minute new business pitch* or *I am giving a twenty-five-minute quarterly review*. This is the wrong way to think about your presentation. Length should be a secondary thought. Making your points come across in an interesting, memorable way is what counts.

Great Hollywood directors know this. James Cameron didn't set out to make a ninety-minute movie about the *Titanic*. Instead, he set out to make the best movie about the *Titanic* that he possibly could. The fact that it was three hours and fourteen minutes long was irrelevant to him. He used as much time as he needed to tell his story about a ship and an iceberg. You need to have the same philosophy with your presentation—even if there is no love story angle.

Yet in almost every training session, I am asked, "How can I be more concise?" I always respond the same way: "Why do you want to be concise?" Typically, people don't have a good answer for this other than some vague, general notion that, all things being equal (they never are), it's better to be concise than it is to be long-winded.

In my experience, most mediocre presenters tend to fixate on the length of a speech because they have a negative mind-set. They want to get through the speech with minimum pain or damage; therefore, they focus on how to make the presentation shorter, faster, leaner, and more concise. This is a horrible and destructive mind-set! It's a mind-set driven by the fact that most business presentations are really, really boring and seem to go on way too long. So, if you have a choice between being really boring for a long time versus being really boring for a short time, then it's better to be really boring for a short time because that will inflict less pain on your audience.

But your goal in presenting shouldn't be as fundamentally negative and depressing as causing the least amount of pain! Here's the fundamental insight about being concise that few people realize: As long as what you are saying is interesting, relevant, helpful, and memorable, then your audience will think you were concise—even if you speak for five hours! However, if you seem to be going through a laundry list of boring facts, data, and numbers, no one will think you are concise—even if you speak for only three minutes.

Of course, there may be times when you are under strict time limitations. For example, you may be presenting at a financial conference where every company is given exactly twenty minutes. Or you may be granted precisely fifteen minutes to make a sales pitch to the general manager of an auto dealership on why she should advertise with your TV station. In these cases, make sure you don't speak longer than the allotted time. And if you want to know how long your presentation is, you must time it when you rehearse. If you read it silently, you'll end up with a severely inaccurate sense of how long your presentation is because you can read much faster than you can speak.

Regardless of the constraints for your presentation, your goal as a presenter must always be to present your key points in a way that is interesting, memorable, useful, and relevant to your audience. That should be your goal—not being concise. When I ask people to tell me about the best presenters in their industry or their company and why they like that person, no one ever says, "I like Jane because she always speaks in a concise manner." They always say things like, "Jane speaks with great passion and always connects with the audience by giving stories and examples they can relate to."

In my experience, people who worship the God of Concision end up hurting themselves and their audiences. When you strive to be concise, the first thing you do is get rid of your relevant stories. The second thing you do is eliminate good examples. The third thing you do is strip out tangible case studies. You are left with a jumble of disconnected, abstract numbers and data points. Sure, you stood up, delivered your concise presentation, and then sat down again without embarrassing yourself, but you didn't actually communicate anything.

Please don't think I am giving you an excuse to ramble or give three-hour tirades the way Fidel Castro used to do to his captive audiences. It's possible to go on and on and be too long. But I have never once in my forty-five years of life heard an audience member turn to someone and say, "I really wish that presenter had NOT told those last interesting, memorable, and useful case studies that will help me make my business grow more effectively." If someone thinks your presentation is too long, chances are you became boring. Therefore, attack the real problem: the boredom, not the length.

Once you realize that presenting is an opportunity to help yourself, your company, and your cause, you won't have a bias toward keeping it short; instead, you will have a permanent bias in favor of being interesting and memorable. And when you have that, the length of your presentation will take care of itself.

TJ TV: Want to captivate audiences just like Martin Luther King, Jr., did? To watch TJ analyze Martin Luther King, Jr.'s, techniques, go to www.tjwalker.com, register if you're a first-time visitor, and enter the words SPEECH TIMING in the TJ TV form.

How many points should I cover in my presentation?

Your marketing director is going to want you to include the top fifteen marketing points. Your sales manager will throw in another ten. Your corporate attorney will want you to add five more to protect yourself. And you will want to show everyone how smart you are by throwing in another thirty-seven. Add them all up and that comes to . . . sixty-two points too many.

The bigger your corporation or organization, the stronger the pull will be to add more and more points to your presentation. There won't be anyone advocating for you to have fewer message points. Everyone will be making a forceful and compelling case to add more messages. There is only one little flaw with this strategy—it doesn't work with audience members.

The Secret

The magic number of points to cover in a presentation is exactly five.

How did I come up with this number?

For the last several years I have asked the following question of my presentation-training clients: "Think of the best speaker you have seen in person in the last year. I'm not talking about a professional motivational speaker or a celebrity like Bill Clinton—just focus on someone in your industry or maybe even your company. Now, how many specific, distinct message points do you remember from that presentation?"

Occasionally, people say: "I can't remember a single thing. I must have a bad memory." Often, they will respond by listing two or three points they still remember. And very, very rarely, someone will be able to summarize a great speaker's five specific key messages.

In all of the years I have been asking my clients this question, guess how many remembered more than five specific message points?

Zero. That's right, not one. And it doesn't matter how educated the audience members are, what industry they are in, or what continent they are from. I work with them all and the responses are always the same.

KEEP YOUR MESSAGE POINTS IN CHECK TO KEEP YOUR AUDIENCE ENTHRALLED.

When I suggest that your presentation should have five points, it's not because five is my lucky number. It really does seem that most adults can remember only five or fewer points from a speech or presentation, even a really good one. And you need to cover one point at a time because your audience is listening to you one point at a time. Make your point, give evidence, give facts, give numbers, and give stories, all to buttress that one point. Then and only then should you try to go to the next point.

Some presenters actually think there are just two options when presenting: either do a thorough, professional job and cover seventy points or do a lazy, half-baked job and cover merely five points. The reality is the exact opposite, as Mark Twain humorously noted: "I didn't have time to write you a short letter, so I wrote you a long one instead." It's actually easier to prepare a speech that has fifty-seven separate message points in it. No tough decisions have to be made about what to put in and what to leave out; what points are the most important and what are the least; which departments are going to be the most angered by your decisions to cut their content. But remember, your audience doesn't care about what is easy for you; they only care about what is easy for them, and it's too darn hard for them to remember fifty-seven new ideas they heard just once!

So much of delivering a foolproof presentation has nothing to do with the mechanics of speaking or the quality of your voice. Instead, it has to do with fundamental judgment. Too many presenters don't use enough judgment as to what messages they are going to cover in their presentation. And if you try to cover fifty-seven or two hundred or anything more than five points, you won't communicate any one of them effectively. And don't think that you can get away with more than 5 and have the audience remember the 1 or 2 that you think are most important. Each individual will remember the points that were most relevant to him or her, and those may or may not be your key points.

Properly viewed, a presentation is a process that you can and should engineer. I'll give you another analogy—and if you're technically minded, this will probably hit home. If you are building an oil pipeline, you would engineer a system so that 100,000 gallons of oil flowing into the pipeline means that 100,000 gallons will flow out hours or days later. You would never say: "Huh, only 50,000 gallons came out the other end. There must be a leak. Oh, well." Instead, you would find the leak and fix it to make sure all 100,000 gallons come out at the end. You'd work all night; you'd spare no expense; you'd work until you got it right.

Unlike engineers and other technical people, many business presenters prepare a presentation with seventy key messages and are happy if, at the end of the process, the audience remembers one or two ideas and comes away with a general feeling that the presenter was competent. This is crazy. You need to decide which five messages you want people to remember and begin the process with a plan for delivering those five messages.

Instead of setting yourself up for failure, you need to write out all of your message points and then prioritize them. Isolate your top five ideas. Those are the ideas you should speak about. You can share all of the other ideas in a handout, in an e-mail, or on a T-shirt—whatever! Just don't talk about more than five points in your actual presentation.

You have to choose: Communicate five points, or communicate absolutely nothing at all. Remember, communication is not what comes out of your mouth, it's what is heard, understood, and remembered by your audience. You can communicate your most important message points every time if you respect and listen to the needs of your audience.

TJ TV: Want to watch John F. Kennedy presenting a big, bold, ambitious message? Go to www.tjwalker.com, register if you're a first-time visitor, and enter the words BOLD MESSAGE in the TJ TV form.

Should I tell 'em what I'm gonna tell 'em, tell 'em, and then tell 'em what I told 'em?

The goal of telling your audience what you're going to tell them, telling them, and then telling them what you told them is to get everyone to remember your messages. This is an excellent goal, and I applaud you for focusing on this particular objective. But at the tactical level, this method isn't very effective. A far more effective technique is to package your messages with interesting and memorable stories, case studies, and examples—and to deliver them with passion and feeling.

Here is the fundamental insight: It doesn't matter if you say something three times or three hundred times. If you say it in a boring and unmemorable manner, no one will ever remember it. If you say something once in a memorable, visual, emotional, specific, relevant way, people will remember what you said minutes, hours, days, even years later.

The Secret
Spend less time focusing on telegraphing the outline of your presentation to your audience and more time simply being interesting.

Take this little test:

Answer quickly: How many emergency exit doors are there on a 737?

Anytime I ask a group of presentation trainees this question, I get answers ranging from two to twelve. Yet anyone who travels has been told exactly how many exit doors there are dozens or even hundreds of times. Somehow, we still don't remember. (Confession: I have no idea how many exit doors there are.) We don't remember how many doors there are on the plane because we are presented with this information while we're getting comfortable, stowing our bags, or looking at the safety brochure. And the information is delivered in such a perfunctory manner, without any effort to get our attention, it's no surprise we can't remember it.

So, why would you think that delivering critical information about your key messages at the very beginning of your presentation is a good idea? Engage your audience first. Get their attention. Then focus on making the delivery of your messages interesting, entertaining, and relevant.

I'm not saying that a quick recap at the end of your presentation won't work in some circumstances, but overall, the tell 'em what I'm gonna tell 'em–tell 'em–tell 'em what I told 'em structure for a presentation just doesn't work.

TJ TV: Want tips to making your presentations more interesting? Go to www.tjwalker.com, register if you're a first-time visitor, and enter the words BEING INTERESTING in the TJ TV form.

How do I know what messages and topics will be most interesting to my audience?

You have three choices:

One, you can guess. The problem is that you won't make a good guess because you are too close to the content. Messages that you consider too obvious to even warrant discussion might well be exactly what your audience is most interested in.

Two, you can "play it safe" by covering every conceivable point you have on the topic. This way, no one can accuse you of leaving out something important or being less than thorough. The problem, of course, is that this isn't safe at all. It's extremely dangerous. When you dump too much data on your audience, you drown out the most important points in your message. Instead of communicating everything, you communicate nothing.

Three, you can pick up a phone and call a couple of people who will be in your audience. Ask them, "What do you think you and your colleagues are most interested in hearing about when it comes to (your topic here)?" In case you didn't notice, this is the right choice.

The Secret

Take a few minutes to call future members of your audience and ask them what they want you to talk about.

When you do this, you send a message loud and clear that you care about your audience and are responsive to their needs and desires. Some presenters are afraid to do this for fear that they won't seem professional and authoritative. But in the end, you will seem more professional if you conduct research on your audience's needs, because your presentation will be far, far better—at least in their eyes, and those are the only ones that matter.

You can use this technique in every setting. Before you have a staff meeting, ask members of your staff to e-mail you their recommendations for topics they would like you to cover. Before you meet with a client team to discuss the status of a project, ask them what particular

ASKING YOUR AUDIENCE NOW WHAT THEY WANT TO HEAR IS BETTER THAN LEARNING LATER THEY WEREN'T INTERESTED IN WHAT YOU CHOSE.

concerns they have that they would like you to address. Before you deliver a speech at a conference, ask the conference organizers what they think the audience will want you to cover.

There's one important thing to keep in mind with this advice: If you ask your audience for input, you have to follow through and actually shape your presentation around what they told you they want to hear.

Calling potential audience members before you speak to them is a free, simple, and easy way to find out exactly what messages you should cover in your presentation and to eliminate the risk of picking wrong or inappropriate topics. The only reason not to call is laziness. And when you display laziness to your audience, they return it in kind. So, pick up the phone and call your audience today! They will love the attention and pay you back accordingly.

TJ TV: Do you have to present the same data over and over? TJ has some video advice to help keep it interesting. Go to www.tjwalker .com, register if you're a first-time visitor, and enter the words REPETITIVE TALK in the TJ TV form.

How should I use humor?

Humor in a presentation is a good thing because if you get audience members to laugh, you know the following things are true:

- They were listening to you and not sleeping!
- They understood you.
- They processed what you said.
- They liked what you said.
- They are communicating back to you in the form of laughter.
- You likely said something unexpected.
- You aren't boring them.
- They like you more because you aren't boring them.

- They aren't sneaking a peek at their cell phones to check text messages.
- You have brightened their day (laughter always does that).

Humor is a good thing, but it is also tricky. Every member of your audience has a different sense of humor, so you have to be cautious. Beware of these pitfalls when using humor:

If you start your speech with a joke, you lose the war on the expected. It's a cliché to start that way. Too many people are expecting it. Half of the effectiveness of humor is being unexpected.

Don't tell canned or generic jokes. If you sound like you are trying to be a comedian, then people will compare you to professional comedians and you will lose.

The sensitivity police are everywhere. Make sure your humor won't be interpreted as mean, nasty, negative, or insensitive.

Your humor needs to have a point; otherwise, you will be seen as just another amateur comedian.

Never preface a joke by saying, "Let me tell you a funny joke." Never preface a funny story by saying, "Let me share a funny story." Don't tell people you are telling a joke or story. Just tell it. Otherwise, you destroy the element of surprise. Plus, the audience wants to decide for themselves whether the joke or story is humorous.

UNLESS YOU HAVE YOUR OWN SITCOM, LEAVE THE TIRED
COMEDY AT HOME.

Never feel like you have to be funny (unless you are a
paid comedian).

Don't look rejected if the audience doesn't laugh when
you think they should laugh.

Don't berate the audience for not laughing.

Don't seem like you are trying to be funny. Don't be a
clown. It just deflates your authority.

After all that, it doesn't seem like I've given you a lot of options for using humor in your presentations. Not true! You still have many options. Your best bet is to follow one key piece of advice.

The Secret
The best thing to do is to retell stories that happened to you that were funny at the time and that still seem funny to others when they hear them.

If your stories and anecdotes are personal, then your humor will be authentic. Plus, if you are making fun of yourself, no one gets offended, and you seem like a class act for being able to poke fun at yourself.

A part of the beauty of humor is that it really increases your audience's ability to remember you and your messages. I still remember North Carolina Secretary of State Thad Eure giving a speech at an American Legion Boys convention in 1980. Eure was speaking to hundreds of U.S. high schoolers who would soon be freshmen in college. He started off with, "I still remember when I was a freshman in college." (He was in his 80s at the time.) "All the upperclassmen were nice enough to call me Freshman Eure [pronounced *fresh manure*]." As you can imagine, that went over very well in a convention hall full of teen-age boys.

As a presenter, you shouldn't try to get a big belly laugh every ten seconds. You aren't a comedian. But there is no reason why you can't steal an effective trick from comedians. If you ever go to comedy clubs, you will see many comedians bring a recording device up to the stage with them. They record their act and then listen to it to see what parts got the biggest laughs and what parts fell flat. You can do the same. Record your presentations and then listen to find out what generated the most laughs. You can use those stories or jokes again and again, as long as they fit with your message and your audience hasn't heard them recently. If something falls flat, chuck it. Don't assume it was a problem with "this audience's sense of humor."

Your goal as a presenter is to communicate messages to get people to act, not to serve as a court jester. But if you can make people laugh, get them to like you, and have them remember some of your messages through the use of humor, you will be way ahead of the competition.

TJ TV: Want to see Bono make fun of himself in a very effective way? Go to www.tjwalker. com, register if you're a first-time visitor, and enter the words BONO HUMOR in the TJ TV form.

Do I have to use stories in my presentation?

Most presenters, including me, would rather not use stories in speeches. Stories take up time, and they are an inefficient way of communicating message points. But here is a central fact of foolproof presentations: Stories work! In fact, as I test audiences all over the world (by simply asking them what they remember from presenters), the only thing that routinely stands out are the stories they heard.

The Secret
Stories are far and away the most effective memory devices for your audience.

I constantly hear things like this: "But TJ, I'm a CFO. My presentation is cut-and-dried. It's all numbers. I can't possibly tell a story. I'd be laughed out of the boardroom!" But the most significant numbers in a quarterly report *do* have a story behind them. Numbers and facts do not speak for themselves. If they did, no one would ever have to give a presentation. Everything has a context and is only meaningful to your audience in that context. Explaining context is why stories are so necessary.

Therefore, if you want somebody to remember an important message, you need to give an example, tell a story, reveal a case study, and perhaps draw a picture or show a photo. Then and only then do you have even a good chance of an audience member remembering something you have said. Among those memory devices, stories are in a league of their own, a league apart from anecdotes and examples. If a certain point is critical, tell a story to support it.

This concept is massively misunderstood by most presenters in the world. Why? Because our role models for presenters are teachers and professors. And most teachers and professors teach by presenting lots and lots of facts, bullet points, and numbers. But here's the rub: Teachers have a very different relationship with their audiences than you probably have with yours.

If I am your college biology teacher and you are my freshman student, I have great power over your life. I can be a boring, data-dumping, droning professor, and guess what, you have to take it. You are a highly motivated audience member. Why? Because I have power over your life. I have the authority to test you in two weeks based on what I am saying in class today. If you fail the test, then you flunk the class. Now you can't go to medical school or graduate school. You lose your financial aid. Your parents stop supporting you. No more parties. Suddenly, there's a direct correlation between remembering what I'm saying and a life of flipping hamburgers for minimum wage and living in a beat-up trailer. Your life is over and I have ruined it.

So, I have the power to motivate you to listen and remember. I might be the most boring professor on campus, but you will still learn a lot of biology. You are learning not because of *how* I presented but in spite of it. (Although I'd be willing to bet that if you had to name your favorite teacher from high school or college, you would likely pick someone who spoke with passion, gave real-world examples, and occasionally told stories.)

It turns out, then, that the biggest role models most of us have as presenters, our teachers, are usually the worst role models we could possibly have because of the different power relationships we have with our audience members versus the teacher-student relationship.

If you are going to make a presentation, it's great to have the command position of authority that professors have. But back in the real world, we almost never have this authority over our audiences. We can't fire our sales prospects if they don't write down everything we say. We can't kick a business partner out of our office for not paying attention. In theory, if you are the CEO of a company, you have the power to fire any employee who doesn't memorize what you've said. But I've asked hundreds of CEOs if they have ever fired an employee for this and no one has ever said yes.

Audiences remember stories and they remember the messages behind stories. Audiences do not remember facts and data delivered in isolation. And no, it doesn't help if you list the facts on a PowerPoint slide so that the audience can see the facts while you are reading them. (However, it is fine to give handouts with lists of facts that people can take with them.)

Let me illustrate. When I am conducting a typical eight-hour training session with a group, I will tell them six industries I work in, six types of clients I work with, and six TV networks I've appeared on. An hour or two later, I will call on one of the trainees to name all eighteen points. This usually results in a nervous chuckle followed by a feeble attempt to name two or three, with one or two usually being wrong. No one ever gets more than five (the magic number) right. Clearly, I have not communicated. In my case, it was by design, to make a point. I remind my audience that I had perfect speaking conditions—everyone had a front row seat, I made sure they had fresh coffee, I was miked for adequate volume—and I'm a professional keynote speaker! And yet, I still failed.

STORIES AREN'T JUST FOR BEDTIME. USE THEM CORRECTLY, AND YOUR MESSAGE WILL STAY WITH YOUR AUDIENCE.

I hope you are skeptical about what I am saying here. In fact, I don't want you to blindly take my word for it. I want you to challenge me. But I also want you to challenge the assumptions you have been going by for years when you make a presentation. Don't take my word for it. Deliver your presentation the old-fashioned way: Start by listing the twelve points you plan to cover and then dump lots of data. Test your audiences. I might be lying to you, but your audience won't. If they don't remember your facts and messages, you failed; your system doesn't work.

Once you realize that delivering information in a straightforward, concise, linear fashion .doesn't really work in presentations (even though a lot of people claim that is what they want in a speaker), it will change everything about how you prepare and deliver presentations for the rest of your life.

TJ TV: Joel Osteen uses stories effectively. See how by going to www.tjwalker.com, register if you're a first-time visitor, and enter the words OSTEEN MOM in the TJ TV form.

How can I be a better storyteller?

When you are making a presentation, your goal is not to develop a reputation as a great storyteller. Instead, your goal is to communicate messages so that people can remember them, act upon them, and tell other people what they are. Stories are simply the most efficient device for helping us get our audiences to remember our messages.

The problem is that people don't know what an effective story in a presentation setting looks like. It's not a story for the sake of a story. It's not a random inspirational tale without relevance to your topic. It's not something you offer just to entertain. It's not something you need to make up or be overly creative with. It's usually neither long nor heavy with emotional impact.

The Secret

To tell a good story in a presentation, relive (don't memorize) a true experience you had that you have an emotional connection with, that your audience cares about and finds relevant, and that is relevant to a specific message point in a clear way.

I realize this doesn't tell you everything you want to know about how to tell a good story, so here are the basic elements of good stories for you to review.

- A setting—physically describe where you were and what you saw
- Characters—preferably you and one other person
- Dialogue—what did you say to that person and what did he/she say to you
- A problem—highlight the point of conflict (every story has one)
- Emotions—describe how you felt, and don't be afraid to be honest
- A clear-cut message for your audience

That's all you need. The reality is that all of us tell stories all day long to friends, family members, and colleagues. We do this one-on-one to make a point or to express ourselves, whether it is to talk about our day in the office, an annoying client, or frustrating traffic.

Here is an example of how to use a story in a business setting. Background: I am giving a media training seminar to a group of executives. I want to convey the message that the training principles I am about to teach them are not based on brilliant insights that I created out of thin air or from academic research but are lessons I learned the hard way, through mistakes. And now they can learn faster and easier than I did. So I begin . . .

I'm not standing before you because I was born knowing how to speak to the media more effectively than anyone else. I've had to learn the hard way. Some of you told me you fear talking to the media because you worry about being quoted out of context. I can relate. Back in 1991 I was working as a press secretary for a member of Congress. One day a reporter calls me up and asks, "TJ, what's the purpose of HR 1400 that your congressman is sponsoring?"

I said, "Currently the legislation is unclear. But it's being cleaned up in committee, and once that happens, people will see it has nothing to do with . . ." I finished the interview and went home to pack for a trip. The next day I was scheduled to fly to Hawaii for a congressional fact-finding mission.

The next day I arrive at the office, suitcase—with swimsuit, suntan lotion, and Hawaiian shirts—in hand. The newspaper's on my desk. I open it up. There's the story on HR 1400. And there I am in the first paragraph: "The spokesperson, TJ Walker, concedes 'the legislation is unclear.'" End of quote. Wait! Where's the rest of it? I start to panic. After the jump, on page B17 near the end of the story is the rest of my quote about how great the legislation will be after it goes through the committee process.

Ugh. I slump in my chair in my little cubicle in the Capitol. Then my phone rings. It's Jim, the congressman's chief of staff. He wants to see me right away.

"TJ, the good news is you're packed. The bad news is you won't be going to Hawaii. But you will be leaving here. The congressman will no longer be in need of your services. Good-bye."

Ouch. I just lost my job.

So, the lessons we work on today are based on the real-world desire that all of us have to keep our jobs. If you follow the techniques I show you, then you won't be out on the street like I was with your bags packed and nowhere to go.

Is that a brilliant story? No. Will it win me a Pulitzer prize? No. But it happens to be true, I deliver it in less than two minutes, it is memorable, and it makes my point. It works! It works because it contains all of the elements I outlined earlier.

You have your own stories. Use them. They might be twenty seconds long or five minutes long. No matter. As long as they meet the big criteria, they're good.

My clients complain, "TJ, I can't think of any good stories." My response is: "You're trying too hard. Be lazy. Just think of a time you had someone call you with a work problem and how you worked it out. Where were you? Spell it out. Who called you? Give the person's name and title. What exactly was the problem? How was it resolved? How did you feel about it?"

Unfortunately, it is practically impossible for you to delegate story creation to staff members or writers in the corporate communications department. Your stories have to come from you. Even someone like President Ronald Reagan, who had a whole team of professional speech-writers, had to write his own stories. The first thing every member of his speech-writing staff did when they were hired was to read old radio and TV commentaries that Reagan personally wrote before he was president. These stories were then recycled within presidential speeches.

The best stories don't require an ounce of creativity or hard work; they just require you to relive an experience you had that is interesting and relevant to other people. Foolproof presenters make it a habit of having a relevant story for each and every message point they plan to communicate in their presentation. If you can't find a story, ask someone else you work with for a story, and give them full credit. If you can't think of a story and you can't find one from anyone else, then maybe it's not such an important point and doesn't deserve a mention in your presentation after all.

TJ TV: Want to watch a video of master storyteller Ronald Reagan at work? Go to www. tjwalker.com, register if you're a first-time visitor, and enter the words REAGAN STORY in the TJ TV form.

Should I make this a formal or an informal presentation?

I often get this question, but I don't really know what it means. There really is no such thing as a formal presentation or an informal presentation—from the perspective of the audience. There are really only two kinds of presentations in the entire world:

Good ones.

Bad ones.

Really. That's it.

Think about when you are listening to someone speak. Are you thinking, "Wow, I sure am glad this presenter is being formal"? Of course not. The audience doesn't think in these terms, so you shouldn't either.

The Secret

Your focus must always be on how you can present your ideas in an interesting, memorable, and conversational way— regardless of your venue, audience size, or subject matter.

There are typically only two possible reactions you, as a presenter, are likely to get from your audience: (1) "Wow, this person is saying something interesting and useful. I'm going to pay attention and tell other people about this." (2) "Uh oh, this presenter is really boring. I'll pretend to pay attention but I'll really be playing with my BlackBerry." Your job is to figure out how to get the first reaction.

The challenge for most presenters is that they often forget this focus and get caught up in trying to figure out what a formal presentation is and whether or not they should give one. But they're usually wrong. Why? Because there is no such thing as a formal or an informal presentation, just a good one or a bad one.

Most presenters confuse setting, length of presentation, and audience size for formality. For you, the presenter, it may feel scarier, and therefore more formal, to speak to a much larger group of people than you usually do. But from any one audience member's perspective, it's still the same—they are listening to one person.

I get very nervous when one of my clients tells me he has to give a formal presentation. Typically, that means he is about to take all of the interesting stories, anecdotes, case studies, humor, pauses, and conversational style that work so well for him and throw them out the window. Then, he replaces all of those dynamic elements with bulleted lists of data that he reads from slides or notes. To make matters worse, he speaks loudly and monotonously—to sound more official. Ugh! This is not a "formal" presentation; it is simply a "bad" presentation.

Ronald Reagan, Bill Clinton, and Tony Blair are—or were—very different speakers with different philosophies, but they are all great speakers. Why? They never let their formal surroundings make them sound "formal." All three spoke in an informal, conversational manner. They didn't change their styles just because the venue changed. Whether they were talking to two people or two million, they still had an informal tone that sounded real, fresh, conversational, and interesting—the opposite of the typical business speaker giving a "formal" speech.

Please remember that it doesn't matter if you are given a strict time limitation or are using PowerPoint or are speaking to a large group of people. Don't tell yourself you are giving a "formal" presentation. Instead, just focus on how you can speak in a conversational tone of voice and convey your ideas in an interesting and memorable manner. Then, from your audience's perspective, you will be delivering a "good" presentation.

TJ TV: Martin Luther King, Jr., was great at connecting with all kinds of audiences in all kinds of settings. See some examples by going to www.tjwalker.com, register if you're a first-time visitor, and enter the words KING CONNECTION in the TJ TV form.

USING POWERPOINT AND VISUALS

Should I use PowerPoint or other technology to enhance my presentation?

That depends. Do you want to use technology to genuinely enhance the learning experience for your audience? Or are you using it as a crutch for yourself because you think it will make it easier for you to give the presentation? Or worse, are you using PowerPoint because everyone else is using PowerPoint and you feel stupid if you don't?

The Secret

Only use PowerPoint or any other technology if it really helps your audience understand and remember your messages more effectively.

You should never *need* to use PowerPoint or any technology. You should be able to communicate your messages effectively simply by talking. Thus, the real question is, Can your audience benefit in any way by seeing some graphic, image, or video of what you are talking about in order to better understand your ideas? If the answer is yes, then you should include some type of visuals in your presentation.

Before you put any given slide or video clip into your presentation, ask yourself these questions:

1. Will this genuinely help my audience understand and remember my points better?
2. What is the worst thing that will happen if I leave this slide or video clip out of my presentation?

For example, I frequently give a keynote speech called "Bully Pulpits: Speaking Secrets of World Famous Leaders." I am certainly capable of giving the speech without any PowerPoint slides or video clips. But I have decided it is much more interesting, insightful, and memorable for my audiences to see short video clips of Reagan, Churchill, Clinton, and Oprah in action rather than just to hear me talk about them. Also, I'm not very good at impersonations. So I have a set of PowerPoint slides that includes video clips.

Presentations that rely on PowerPoint slides often have a well-deserved reputation for being dreadful, but not because there is anything inherently wrong with the program. All of the flaws associated with PowerPoint flow from one fundamentally flawed decision the presenter made before the presentation started. Namely, that the presenter decided to use PowerPoint as a crutch for herself, not as an actual aid for the audience. Once the decision is made to use visual elements and technology in a way that is truly helpful to the audience, most of the problems associated with PowerPoint or other forms of technology disappear.

Too many executives and salespeople automatically gravitate toward the high-tech solution to presentations. Video can now be inserted into a PowerPoint presentation, but it is not easy for most people to do. If you are going to use video, you also have to make sure you have the right plug-ins on your computer, you have to have speakers, and you have to be sure that the projector can handle it. You can't just store the presentation on a CD or memory stick and assume it will work on someone else's laptop. I estimate that 75 percent of the presenters I see who attempt to use video can't get it to work, and they end up mumbling a bunch of apologies. I use video clips in every one of my presentations because I am speaking about speaking, hence I need to show great examples of people speaking. But too many people want to use a video clip for no apparent reason other than to show off or because technology lets them—both of which are terrible reasons.

If you are going to use PowerPoint or other technology in your presentations, you must realize that it is a big commitment. You need more rehearsal. There will be many more moving parts that can go wrong. Ultimately, it is your responsibility if people cannot see your slides or if there is no audio coming out of your speakers or if the projector won't work with your laptop. Nothing is more feeble than a speaker complaining to the audience about bad audio, an out-of-date projector, or lack of wireless connection. You don't hear Mick Jagger complaining about his lighting or sound system when he is performing in front of 90,000 people in a stadium. Why? Because he got to the stadium six hours earlier to do a rehearsal and sound check. If it's good enough for Mick, it's good enough for you. You are both in the business of providing satisfaction to your audience.

One thing that you must realize is that you will never give a "PowerPoint presentation." There is no such thing as a PowerPoint presentation. PowerPoint is simply one tool to help things along. You aren't giving a PowerPoint presentation any more than you are giving an electricity presentation. Granted, electricity is nice to have, especially during a presentation. But electricity is just a helper, just as your PowerPoint slides or other learning tools are. You aren't fundamentally giving an electricity presentation.

What you are giving is an "audience-focused Tom presentation" or an "audience-focused Meg presentation."

Because your audience will judge you and your content, not Microsoft for developing PowerPoint, make sure you are using it or any other technology for all the right reasons.

TJ TV: Get more tips on using PowerPoint effectively. Go to www.tjwalker.com, register if you're a first-time visitor, and enter the words POWERPOINT TIPS in the TJ TV form.

What do I really need to know about PowerPoint in order to use it effectively?

There are 20,465 books on PowerPoint for sale on Amazon.com, which means that there are more than four million pages of content you could read to learn about how to use all the bells and whistles of PowerPoint! You don't have to read them all. In fact, if you just follow the ten tips below, you will consistently be the most effective user of PowerPoint anyone in your audience has ever seen.

1. Create two separate sets of PowerPoint slides: one for projecting on a screen, and one to both e-mail to audience members in advance and hand out after your presentation. Your e-mail/print PowerPoint slides can be jam-packed with words, numbers, text, data points—make it two hundred pages if you like.

(Note that Tips number 2 through 10 apply just to the PowerPoint slides you are projecting.)

2. Use images, charts, pictures, video clips, or any other visual element.

3. Focus on one idea per slide. One means "one." It doesn't mean cram four charts that cover the same basic topic onto one slide.

4. Don't use ANY text. This is not a typo. You can call me insane. You can complain that your corporate culture demands that you use text. I'm telling you, text doesn't work when you are projecting on a screen twenty, thirty, or fifty feet away from people. This is not how human beings like to read.

5. Use as many slides as you need.

6. Don't use any slide unless it makes your idea more clear and memorable than you simply saying it.

7. If you want people to look at your slide, then stop talking long enough for them to do so.

8. If you want people to listen to you, then don't have a slide up behind you to distract them.

9. Remember, you are the star of the presentation, not the PowerPoint slides.

10. You aren't prepared to use PowerPoint unless you can give the whole presentation without the ability to show the slides (because projectors and computers can malfunction).

That's really all you need to know about PowerPoint. To help you understand a few of these rules even better, I'll elaborate a bit.

Please note that I clearly said that you have to have TWO separate sets of PowerPoint slides. If you have just one set with photos and images, then you can and will be attacked for being fluffy, superficial, nonsubstantive, and incomplete. You MUST have the second set. This one is to be e-mailed to people (preferably in advance, but it could be sent out after the presentation too) and to be printed out and handed to them so that they can read it when they have the time. If you prepare both sets of slides and the nonprojected version has all of the data, numbers, and facts that anyone could ever want, then you protect yourself from criticism and you help people by giving them a true resource that they can refer back to weeks or months later.

There are a lot of smart, successful people in the world who will tell you that you must follow specific rules for creating a set of PowerPoint slides, such as use ten slides and three bullet points each and three words per bullet point. Nevertheless, these rules don't work! (Though some of them will make your presentation less painful than the typical data dump.) I have personally tested audiences all over the world for years and the only thing anyone ever remembers are slides with visual elements. No one ever remembers words.

The Secret

Your audience will remember your message better if you give them visual cues to help them, not a bunch of text on a screen.

What works in one medium does not work necessarily in another medium. You might love reading Harry Potter, but if you went to the movie theater to watch a Harry Potter movie, you'd probably be pretty angry if all you saw was text moving across the movie screen for twenty-seven hours. Most business executives would never think of taking the text from a newspaper ad and turning it into a television ad, yet for some reason we think that text on our computer should work fine projected on a screen a long way away from people. It doesn't work that way.

Our brains are better image processors than they are word processors. What is easier for you to remember when you pass someone on the street that you met a month before: the spelling of their first and last name from their business card, or their face? The person's face, of course. Chances are you recognize the person but you have forgotten his or her name. The face is an image and that is what sticks in the memory.

Now, not every image is a good or an effective image. The rule to follow is this: the simpler the better. The typical PowerPoint graph has eight different lines, all in different colors showing weekly sales results on three continents over the last twelve months. Yes, the graph fits on one slide, but it took you two hours to create it, and now you expect the audience to understand it by looking at it from a distance for sixty seconds while you are talking to them. Ridiculous! Some people get too complicated with their

SOMETIMES IT'S BEST TO LEAVE THE SPECIAL EFFECTS TO HOLLYWOOD.

PowerPoint tricks for the slides that are projected. (It's fine to have a PowerPoint slide with eight color-coded variables as a handout because it can be studied and examined at the convenience of the reader.)

And, while I love PowerPoint, I want to make it clear that what we're really talking about here is effective visual memory enhancers. You shouldn't use slides just because it's convenient. If you are talking about the problem of oranges freezing, don't show a slide of a frozen orange. Bring in a frozen orange, hold it up, and then pass it around.

There is nothing worse than a bad presentation with bad PowerPoint slides, but there is nothing better than a great presenter who uses PowerPoint effectively. Most people use their PowerPoint slides as the poor man's teleprompter. The foolproof presenter uses PowerPoint for the sole benefit of his or her audience.

TJ TV: Want a demonstration of the best ways to use PowerPoint? Go to www.tjwalker.com, register if you're a first-time visitor, and enter the words BETTER PPT in the TJ TV form.

Is it okay to use white-boards, flip charts, and other non-high-tech tools for presentations?

Yes. It's often much better than using overly complicated PowerPoint slides. These low-tech tools are especially effective when you are presenting to groups smaller than fifty and in rooms where everyone can see you clearly.

The Secret
The secret to using any visual tool, and particularly low-tech tools, is simplicity.

The beauty of using a whiteboard or even an old-fashioned chalkboard is that you can draw only one line or one arrow or one thing at a time. This slows you down, which is good because your audience can focus on just one thing at a time. If you are drawing a diagram or chart, live, in front of your audience, it forces you to simplify and to focus on one or two variables alone. This makes it much easier for your audience to grasp what you are talking about.

Another benefit to using a whiteboard, flip chart, or chalkboard is that it forces you to stay away from excessive abstraction. By drawing something, you are focusing on a thing, not just a concept. This helps make your message more concrete for your audience.

When President Reagan wanted to make a point in his State of the Union address that the federal tax code was out of control, he didn't use a PowerPoint slide that showed statistics on the tax code or how long it was in terms of pages or words. He took the actual tax code books, which were as thick as a dozen Manhattan phone books, and dropped them in front of the lectern for all the world to see. It was a dramatic use of a prop that made his point about the complexity of the tax code in a highly memorable way, which people recall even decades after it happened.

It's also important to consider how low-tech tools force you to interact with your environment. They require you to move around, draw, or gesture, and that creates visual diversity and interest and wakes up your audience a bit. If you are prone to being stiff during your presentations, you might want to consider using one of these tools to force you to move around, to interact physically with your environment, and to give your readers something interesting to look at.

Another type of low-tech support to consider is a physical prop. Let's say you were talking about credit card payments being an important new method for interacting with your customers. A photograph of a credit card is better than just printing the text "credit cards" on a slide, but pulling a credit card out of your wallet and holding it up while you make your point about convenience can really send the point home. If you have ever been to a Don Shula steak house, you know the waiter does not just explain the daily specials and hand out a menu with football pictures on the cover. At these restaurants, the menu is printed on an actual football, and that creates a permanent memory for every customer. Props work especially well with audiences of twenty or fewer.

Regardless of whether you use a high-tech tool, a low-tech tool, or an old-fashioned prop, always make your decisions based on what will help your audience understand the most, learn the most, and remember the most.

TJ TV: Want more low-tech tips? Go to www.tjwalker.com, register if you're a first-time visitor, and enter the words LOW TECH in the TJ TV form.

DELIVERING YOUR PRESENTATION

How should I ask to be introduced?

irst impressions count. The first impression of you as a presenter is not formed when you start presenting; it's formed when you are being introduced. It's important that you don't lose your audience before you even get a chance to speak. Don't start off by boring your audience with a lot of details they don't care about. They'll assume that's what your presentation is going to be like and you'll be fighting an uphill battle right from the start. Most audience members are savvy enough to know that you had a hand in how you were introduced.

The Secret

When preparing your introduction, follow two rules: keep it relevant and keep it brief.

When coming up with your introduction, start by asking yourself, "What does the audience need to know about me in order to be interested in what I am about to say and to see me as a credible source on this topic?" Really focus on that. Don't use a generic one-page bio from your Web site or the resume you used to land your last job. You should come up with a uniquely tailored intro for each audience you talk to.

This probably means that your audience doesn't have to know that you were president of the honor society in eleventh grade or that your cat's name is Spooky. Give your audience only the most relevant information and the most interesting information about your background and accomplishments to whet their appetites for your actual messages. If they want your full bio, they can go to your Web site.

Keep in mind that what looks like a quick read on paper can seem interminably long and boring to an audience listening to someone introduce you. If you are giving a one-on-one sales presentation to a single prospective customer, you will be introducing yourself, so it's best to keep it to one or two sentences. If you are speaking in front of a larger group and someone else is introducing you, the introduction could be as long as a minute—but that's still brief. A rough word count to shoot for is between 60 and 160 (the average person speaks 160 words per minute).

IT NEVER HURTS TO HAVE A FEW EXTRA COPIES OF YOUR INTRODUCTION ON HAND.

A separate but related question is how do you actually get your introducer to use the intro you wrote? Try the following:

Type out your intro in bullet-point format in gigantic 20-point type so that it fills an entire sheet of paper, but no more than a single sheet of paper, and e-mail that to the introducer in advance. This makes it easy for your introducer to read it without having to bend close to the paper.

When you get to the venue where you are speaking, hand the introducer a second copy of your introduction. Don't ever assume the introducer will bring what was sent.

Keep a third copy of your introduction handy in your pocket so that when the introducer tells you twenty seconds before he is about to introduce you that he has lost the script, you can give him another one.

Although these are minor details, they can add up nevertheless to make a big impact on your audience. Take the time to do it right.

TJ TV: Want to know the best way to introduce yourself when speaking to a group? Go to www.tjwalker.com, register if you're a first-time visitor, and enter the words SELF INTRODUCTION in the TJ TV form.

How do I connect with my audience?

This is a huge question that every presenter must answer. Unfortunately, most presenters never connect because they decide from the beginning to focus on themselves, not their audience. They think: *This is about MY speech. MY time. MY slides. MY outline. MY lectern. MY handouts.*

This is completely the wrong approach. Foolproof presenters focus entirely on their audience, whether it is an audience of one or one thousand, and this focus is the first step to establishing a connection that could lead to a great presentation. Just as presenters make decisions, so, too, do audiences. And your audience is going to decide very quickly whether they think you care more about helping them or about making yourself look good.

The Secret
Send repeated signals to your audience that you care about them in a genuine and authentic manner.

In my experience, if the audience senses you are concentrating on them, they will listen harder to you, remember more, and have a more positive impression of you, even if you are a less-than-perfect speaker. To let your audience know that you are truly focused on helping them and connecting with them, try the following:

- Start by saying something interesting to the audience, not something about yourself.
- Encourage people to ask you questions at any time.
- Ask questions of your audience.
- Look individual audience members in the eye.
- Look at audience members to see whether they understand what you are saying and are following you.
- Seek verbal and nonverbal agreement occasionally from audience members and comment on it.
- Walk around the room from time to time to get physically close to different audience members.
- Weave in snippets of conversation with audience members that occurred right before the presentation started.

- Use notes in a subtle way that doesn't draw the audience's attention to what you're doing.
- Move out from behind the lectern; literally lean forward into the audience from time to time.
- Respond to both positive and negative reactions from the audience.

I have seen presenters who had their shirt tails hanging out, said lots of "uhs" and "ums," used bad grammar, had ugly PowerPoint slides, and lost their focus, but audiences loved them because they were clearly focused on helping their listeners. On the other hand, I have seen speakers who were impeccably dressed, had strong, powerful voices, and never uttered a single verbal tic, but they fell flat with their audiences because they seemed to be focused on themselves.

You can connect with each and every audience you present to, but this requires a specific focus. Once you decide you care more about your audience than you do about yourself, many things in your delivery will change for the better.

TJ TV: Want to see and learn how John F. Kennedy connected with his audience? Go to www.tjwalker.com, register if you're a first-time visitor, and enter the words JFK CONNECTION in the TJ TV form.

Should I read my speech so that I don't make any mistakes?

No. I plead with you, please do not try to read your presentation.

You may be thinking something like this: "This presentation is really crucial, and I want to get it just right. I don't want to screw up. I'll be speaking to an important audience and I'm going to be nervous. I'm afraid I might forget something." I can sympathize with your thinking, but there are some serious flaws with the reasoning here.

The Secret
Reading a speech is actually an extraordinarily difficult thing to do well— it's not for amateurs.

While it is true that reading is a basic skill mastered by most second graders, reading a speech in front of a roomful of people is extremely difficult and is mastered by very few. Here's why:

- Your speaking speed becomes consistent, which destroys your attempts at a conversational tone.
- Your volume becomes consistent.
- You don't vary your pauses.
- You lose eye contact with your audience.
- You can't see what your audience is reacting to positively or negatively.
- You become monotone.
- Everyone falls asleep.
- You communicate nothing.
- Are you convinced yet?

When an amateur presenter announces that she is planning to read a speech, it strikes me as absurd as a life-long coach potato announcing that he wants to take up exercise, and he is going to start by climbing Mt. Everest! Sure, some trained experts can reach the top of Everest, but an amateur would die trying.

Network news anchors like Charlie Gibson and Brian Williams can read a presentation from a teleprompter and make it sound natural, but not because they were born with this skill. They can do it because they have done it every day for the last quarter of a century—and they still practice.

LEARNING TO READ YOUR SPEECH WITHOUT SOUNDING MECHANICAL
IS MORE DIFFICULT THAN YOU MIGHT THINK.

Ronald Reagan was a master at being able to read a speech and make it sound authentic and believable. Many people erroneously believe that Reagan could do this because of skills he acquired as an actor. But it was really a matter of discipline, not skill. Most people don't realize how much work Reagan put into delivering a major speech. Take the State of the Union address. For starters, Reagan would work intimately with his speech-writers on various drafts of his speech over a period of months. Next, he would read the finished speech out loud for three hours every night for a week. Then, he would spend the entire day the speech was to be delivered doing videotaped rehearsals. It's important to remember that he wasn't doing this to memorize the speech. He was still reading the speech from the teleprompter.

Reagan put all of this time and effort into speech preparation because he realized it's not just the words that count, it's how you deliver them. Reagan's goal was to read the words in such a way that you were never conscious or aware of him reading. Instead, you as the audience member could focus on the meaning of his words and get the sense that Reagan really believed them.

If you still want to read your speech, be my guest, but are you willing to put in as much rehearsal time as Reagan did?

I didn't think so.

Reading full texts is difficult, dangerous, and unnecessary. Instead, just rely on notes.

TJ TV: Learn from the best! Even Winston Churchill used notes. To watch an example, go to www.tjwalker.com, register if you're a first-time visitor, and enter the words CHURCHILL NOTES in the TJ TV form.

How do I remember what to say in a presentation?

Cheat. I'm serious. You need to cheat.

The reality is that it's hard work to memorize a presentation. If you are like me, you already have enough hard work in your life, so let's not add to the list. Don't waste time memorizing. But you need a solution for remembering all of your key points that is easy for you and also helps your audience. You reading a speech word for word is easy for you, but it creates a painful and boring experience for your audience—not a win-win solution.

The Secret
The best tool you can use to help you remember the points you want to make is a really good set of notes, used skillfully.

But even notes have their potential flaws, so you must use them in a very specific way in order for your audience to see you as believable, authentic, and authoritative. I never give a presentation anywhere without using notes, but I create the illusion that I'm not using notes. How is this done? It's easy if you follow these simple rules:

- Limit your notes to a single sheet of paper.
- Use print that is so large that you can read it from five feet away.
- Use one- to four-word sentence fragments to jar your memory.
- Number your points; don't create an outline using complex indentation and subsections.
- Cut your sheet of paper in half so that it is only 4¼ x 11 rather than 8½ x 11; it will be even less noticeable.
- Never pick up your notes.
- Never be seen holding your notes.
- Never be seen touching your notes.
- Have two or three copies of the same notes in different parts of the room so that you don't have to be near any one copy for long stretches of time.
- Know what you want to say the first couple of minutes without having to look at your notes.
- Whenever possible, place your notes in the venue before the audience even enters the room.

- Place your notes on a flat surface such as a table or on the keyboard of your computer.
- Don't make sudden head movements to look down at your notes.
- Don't make quick eye darts down to your notes.
- Move around the room and look at your notes as part of your natural movement.
- Look at your notes when your audience is looking elsewhere, such as the second you show a new slide from a PowerPoint.
- Place one copy of your notes on the table where your water glass or bottle is. Look at your notes when you appear to be just taking a sip of water.
- If a lectern is available, place your notes on the side of it rather than in the normal position. This way you can glance at your notes without ever walking squarely behind the lectern, thus furthering the illusion that you aren't using notes.
- Make sure you have a strong conclusion that you can deliver without having to glance at your notes.

Audiences love it when the person presenting to them appears to be speaking right to them and is not beholden to or reading from a script or notes. Have you ever read a news article about a political or business figure in which the reporter wrote something like, "She spoke for an hour to the mesmerized crowd without using notes." Audiences seem to respect and admire a presenter who doesn't use notes because it seems like a courageous act, like walking across a tightrope without using a safety net. But here's the thing: Audiences don't really care whether or not you use notes, as long as they don't notice you doing so.

If you use the techniques I've outlined here when using notes, it will be almost undetectable, and your audience will think you are one of the best presenters they've seen.

TJ TV: If President Franklin Delano Roosevelt could use notes, so can you! Go to www.tjwalker.com, register if you're a first-time visitor, and enter the words **FDR NOTES** in the TJ TV form.

Should I take questions during my presentation or ask people to hold them until the end?

Some experts advise holding all questions until the end. Others advise answering every single question—no matter how irrelevant—even if that means you never get to your main points. Neither approach works—at least not from the audience's perspective.

The presentation you give belongs to your audience. This is a learning experience for them, not for you. Every decision you make as a presenter has to be geared toward helping the audience. This is why, in most circumstances, I favor letting audience members ask questions at any time. In the following pages I describe how to use the relevant questions, as well as how to move away from other questions that are off topic.

The Secret

When you allow your audience to ask questions at any time, the presentation becomes an engaging, collaborative experience, which creates a great learning environment.

Obviously, if you are speaking to a large crowd of five hundred people or more, you cannot stop every two seconds to take a question; you will have to take questions at the end of your presentation. But chances are that during a typical month you have a lot more opportunities to speak to one, ten, or twenty people at a time. When you are speaking to smaller audiences, you are much better off letting people ask questions at any time.

Average and mediocre presenters take a very dim view of questions. Consequently, they ask audiences to hold their questions until the end of the presentation. This approach is based on six faulty assumptions: (1) Audience questions are interruptions. (2) The questions will interrupt my flow or make me lose my train of thought. (3) Taking questions will disrupt my carefully planned order. (4) I will look like an idiot if I can't answer the questions. (5) If I take time to answer questions, I won't be able to cover all of my important points. (6) I know best what my audience needs to focus on. The problem with all of these assumptions is that they are based on the premise that the presentation is a concrete thing that is owned and operated for the benefit of the presenter. Wrong!

This is a destructive attitude. Instead, your attitude should be, "Great, now someone wants to help me make this an even better presentation and is willing to do part of the work." A foolproof presenter has the same attitude toward questioners that Tom Sawyer had toward recruiting kids to help him paint his fence. Like Tom, the foolproof presenter realizes that the more people who are in on the project, the less time and energy it will take to finish the job.

If you allow people you are presenting to to ask you questions at any time, the following good things are generally true:

- You know that at least one person you are speaking to is paying attention and is not sleeping, daydreaming, or doodling.

- The questioner is trying to process and reflect upon what you are talking about.

- The questioner may be helping you by asking a question that everyone else in the room is thinking.

- The questioner may be forcing you to fill in a gap in your knowledge or logic that everyone else in the room needs in order to understand what you're saying.

- When you answer the question, you know with 100 percent certainty that you are covering messages that are of extreme interest to some of your audience.

- The questioner has provided the audience with some audio variety because now people get to hear two voices instead of just yours.

- The questioner has provided some visual variety because now people in the audience can look at somebody other than you. They may even have to move to see the person, which will wake them up physically.

- The questioner really appreciates you answering the question.

- Audience members are impressed that you are willing to share the spotlight with others.

- Audience members are impressed that you can think on your feet and don't mind being interrupted.

- If an audience member asks an insightful question, you look good by giving an insightful answer.

- If an audience member asks a dumb question, you look classy by answering it patiently (of course, the person asking the question doesn't see it as dumb).

- The whole presentation goes from being a potentially boring lecture where you are in control 100 percent of the time to more of a communal experience in which everyone feels a part of a positive outcome.

Once your attitude has switched to viewing questioners as adding to a collaborative process, your presentation
gets easier, not harder. I know it sounds touchy-feely to
talk about how the whole room is working together, but
the presentation really does work better that way.

There are some limits to taking questions, however.
If someone persists in asking more than two questions or
launches into a series of questions, you can politely say the
following: "I'd like to give your questions the full attention they deserve. If you could meet right here immediately
after the presentation I will go into more detail with you
on that. Thanks." And then move on. But be sure to be
available after the presentation. Remember, too, that even
though you want to encourage questions, you must also
be a strict traffic cop. If someone asks a question that is
off topic, gently but quickly tell him you will speak to him
directly after your presentation is over.

Give your questioners a chance, and odds are they will
add to your presentation and make it better. Once you realize that, you will turn what you used to see as an irritant or
a distraction into your new secret weapon.

TJ TV: Get great tips for the best way to deal
with questions from your audience. Go to
www.tjwalker.com, register if you're a first-time
visitor, and enter the words AUDIENCE Q&A in
the TJ TV form.

What should I do with my hands?

This is one of the most common questions I am asked. People complain to me every week, "I don't know what to do with my hands!"

Somewhere, long ago, it was written that a professional presenter should not move his or her hands when speaking. This is utter nonsense!

The Secret

Use your hands the way you use them all day long when you are talking to one person—move them around to punctuate or illustrate your points.

If you attempt to stop moving your hands when you speak, you set off the following negative chain reaction:

Your body looks literally stiff.

You look uncomfortable.

Your arms stiffen.

Your vocal chords stiffen.

You speak in a lower volume.

You speak monotonously.

You seem more boring.

Don't do it!

In theory, it is possible to move your hands too much and to gesticulate so wildly that you distract your audience. But in a quarter of a century of coaching people around the world, I have never had a client who moved his or her hands too much. Yet every week, sometimes every day, I have clients who freeze their hands or hold pens or grab lecterns to keep their hands from moving.

Let's focus on the real problem, then: When you are nervous, you tense your body and stop moving your hands. This makes you look nervous to the audience, and that's a problem. We want to look natural, relaxed, and confident to our audiences so they can focus on what we are saying, not on what we are doing or not doing with our bodies.

The first thing that usually happens when my clients rehearse in front of a video camera for the first time is they stop moving their hands in a natural manner. They

| THE FIG LEAF | THE CONVICT |

FEEL FREE TO MOVE YOUR HANDS DURING YOUR PRESENTATIONS . . . UNLESS YOU ACTUALLY DO NEED TO USE THE RESTROOM.

will hold their hands in a fig leaf position as if they have to go to the bathroom. Or they hold their hands behind their back in the military at-ease position and it looks like they are about to be arrested. Or they hold on to a pen as if they are about to say something so spontaneously brilliant that they might have to write down their own quote. Or they grab hold of the lectern as if it were a life raft. All of these things make them look uncomfortable and uncertain.

When we are watching a video of a rehearsal, I will ask the trainee what she thinks. The response is usually, "I seem a little flat, boring, and stiff."

Then I ask, "Have you ever thought about moving your hands a little?"

She responds, "Oh, no, TJ, I never move my hands when I speak." Of course, while the trainee is saying this, she is gesturing with wide sweeps and chops, moving both her hands and her arms! Fortunately, I am secretly taping her.

Next I ask: "How would you like to see someone who could be a role model for you? Someone I think you can relate to, but who moves naturally and seems much more confident and comfortable than you do?"

The trainee says yes, thinking that I am about to show a video clip of a great speaker like Barack Obama or Tony Robbins. Instead, I show the video of the trainee herself from moments before. "Which presenter do you like better?" I ask.

This always produces a laugh; but more important, it creates a breakthrough. She prefers her natural way of speaking, which makes her realize that her natural way of speaking is fine. She doesn't need to learn some new theatrical skill to use when presenting in front of people. All she needs to do is to stop acting and to move naturally.

This approach can take some practice. When you are speaking to a new group of people for the first time, or if you are doing anything that takes you out of your comfort zone, you may need to consciously think while speaking, "I am now moving my right hand . . . now I am moving my left hand . . ." You have to prime the pump at the beginning of your presentation by forcing your hands to move. This sounds phony and contrived, but if you practice it, you will look natural and relaxed. And eventually you won't have to remind yourself to move.

Around the world, I find that most audiences respond best to presenters who talk and move in a natural manner. And most people move both hands when they speak. Yes, there are a few exceptions (such as in Japan where it is considered rude to gesture when giving a business presentation). Always try to find out if there are local customs that supersede your own practices, and then follow those local customs. But in general, your audience will see you as confident, authoritative, and authentic if you move your hands when you present.

TJ TV: Watch Hillary Clinton demonstrate how best to use your hands naturally and effectively during a speech. Go to www.tjwalker .com, register if you're a first-time visitor, and enter the words HILLARY HANDS in the TJ TV form.

Who or what should I look at when presenting?

Look at individual audience members, one at a time. This will make you seem comfortable, confident, authoritative, and credible—even if you are scared to death inside.

The following are things you should NOT look at when you are presenting:

The tops of people's heads
The clock
The floor
Your PowerPoint slides
Your fully written script

There are three main categories of eye contact most presenters display. The bottom 5 percent of presenters stare at their notes, their slides, and their shoes—anything but at their audience. This is the worst thing you can do.

The next 94.9 percent do some variation of the "windshield wiper." They look at their audience, but they sweep their gaze back and forth from one side of the room to the other, perhaps quickly, perhaps slowly. This windshield wiper effect doesn't give any one audience member the feeling that the presenter is speaking directly to him or her. No one audience member ever gets eye contact for more than one second because the speaker is looking at the group and not at an individual.

The top 0.1 percent of presenters use their eyes in a way that is very different from the first two groups.

The Secret
Great presenters will pick one specific person in the audience and maintain eye contact with that person for one full thought.

This may be for only five or six seconds, but it is long enough for the audience member to really feel a personal connection with the speaker. The presenter will do this with as many people as possible in the room. The presenter will not play favorites with friends or pretty people or people in the front row. Instead, everyone in the room will get personal eye contact. When the presenter is zeroing in on one person at a time, this gives that presenter the feeling of having a close, personal, intimate conversation with just one other person. This creates a very powerful connection between the audience members and the speaker.

This skill is not hard in the same sense that learning how to be a brilliant composer is hard, but it isn't natural either. It's natural to look at someone you are speaking to for just a couple of seconds and then break eye contact. It's natural when you are standing in front of people to have your eyes dart nervously back and forth across the room. So it will take some practice to master this high level of sustained eye contact.

If you are giving a presentation to only one person in the room, then this rule doesn't apply. It might freak the person out. But if you are standing and presenting to more than a couple of people, it is a highly effective technique.

This also works for extremely large audiences as well. Let's say you are speaking to a convention hall of two thousand people. You are on a stage in the spotlight and the audience is in the dark. You can't even see their faces. Here is what you do: Just pick one spot in the crowd and look right at that spot for a full thought, even though you can't see anything. The effect on the audience will be just as powerful. The twenty or so people in that general area will all feel like you are speaking directly to them. After about six seconds, look to another part of the crowd. Continue to mix it up. Don't look around the room in a clockwork rotation. Instead, look at the front left, then the back left, then the middle of the room. You don't want to look mechanical or like you are moving in a set pattern.

Your eyes are a very powerful tool. By looking directly at an audience member for five or six seconds, you will occasionally make someone uncomfortable. That's okay. Better to make them slightly uncomfortable than to make them so comfortable they fall asleep. Remember, you aren't being rude because you aren't singling anyone out and you are giving equal attention to everyone. If you are speaking for twenty minutes to a room of fifty people, you can give each person individualized eye contact several times during the course of your presentation.

In a subtle way, your eye contact is also conditioning your listeners to be better, more attentive audience members. We have all seen presenters so focused on their slides or notes that they wouldn't notice if an audience member in the first row fell over, had a heart attack, and died on the spot. As audience members, it is only natural for us to ignore presenters when we feel they are ignoring us. But when someone is looking right at us, we feel as though that presenter can tell whether we are paying attention. We as audience members start to focus on the presenter because the direct eye contact makes us feel there is a chance he or she might call on us with a question at any time.

The final benefit to holding eye contact like this is that even to the people who don't have eye contact with you at any given moment, you will seem much steadier and less jerky than most speakers who have their heads bobbing and weaving around.

There is only so much a presenter can do with his or her content to make it more interesting, but when you couple great content with great eye contact, the result is a much more powerful effect on everyone in the room.

TJ TV: Martin Luther King, Jr., was a master at making eye contact with his audience. To watch an example, go to www.tjwalker.com, register if you're a first-time visitor, and enter the words EYE CONTACT in the TJ TV form.

Should I move around the room or stand behind a lectern?

Some experts will advise you to stand still with both feet planted firmly, or to grab the lectern with both hands so that you don't appear shaky. This is terrible advice! You could stand in one spot for your whole presentation and still be a competent presenter, but you run the risk of making yourself seem ordinary and boring if you do.

You are normally better off if you can walk around when you are presenting. This is true whether you are speaking to a group of five or five thousand. Obviously, if you are presenting to just one or two people and they are seated, you can stay seated too. But if you are standing before a larger group, then I recommend that you move around the room.

First, let's address the issue of the lectern. In my view, a lectern should be approached like a set of training wheels—

not something to be used by anyone over five years old. Why? Because the second you get behind a lectern it creates a barrier between you and your audience. It obscures two-thirds of your body. Once you are behind the lectern, you will be tempted to lean on it, hold it, or hold your notes. This means you have shut down all of your natural hand movements. The result is that you come off as a frozen, stiff automaton.

When you stand behind a lectern, you run the risk of making your audience think that you are insecure. It's as if you are hiding behind a wall because you fear the audience is going to turn on you and start throwing rotten vegetables at you!

Why do we get behind lecterns in the first place? Because the person speaking before us did, and the person presenting after us probably will, so it must be the right thing to do, right? Wrong. Your goal as a foolproof presenter is to distinguish yourself as better, more confident, more comfortable, more conversational, more interesting, and more memorable than all other presenters. You can't do that if you follow the pack. I'm not suggesting that you do anything showy or theatrical, but I have found that audiences respond much better to presenters who move around the room.

Professional speakers never use lecterns for this very reason. Even though you might not aspire to become a full-time professional speaker, there is no reason why you can't borrow some of the easy techniques they use. I

MOVING AROUND DURING YOUR PRESENTATION KEEPS THE AUDIENCE FOCUSED ON YOU, NOT THEIR E MAIL OR CELL PHONE.

am constantly amazed that audiences around the world seem to be genuinely impressed when a speaker can walk around a room or stage while speaking. All it is is walking and talking at the same time, something most of us master at three years of age!

Most people have a huge fear of presenting and public speaking; they are afraid they will forget what they are going to say and look like a fool. Therefore, when they see you walking around the room talking to them without staring at notes or holding on to a lectern, there is a part of them that says, "Wow, that presenter is brave; I could never do that!"

Why else do people get behind lecterns? That's often where they store notes. As mentioned in the chapter on remembering what to say during a presentation, you can place notes on the side of a lectern, so that you can look at them without standing directly behind it.

Other times people stand behind the lectern because the microphone is attached to it. Make sure you truly need the microphone. I've seen presenters talk to a room with ten people in it for ten minutes standing behind the lectern and using the microphone. You should just walk right up to the ten people and speak; you don't need a microphone in this setting. If you are in front of a large audience and you need the microphone, you can normally bend the mic stand to the side so that you can stand next to the lectern rather than directly behind it. This way your whole body will be visible. If you are giving a presentation to a large annual sales conference, you should always ask for a wireless microphone so that you won't have to be stuck standing near the lectern. You might not get one, but you won't know unless you ask.

When you are moving around the room, there are a few guidelines to keep in mind.

- Don't walk consistently from side to side or back to front. If your movement is consistent, you will appear to be pacing, and that will make you seem nervous.
- Move naturally, which means inconsistently.
- Feel free to stop moving at any time.
- Move to show you have finished a thought and are taking a moment to signify a transition.
- Move closer to someone when that person asks a question.
- Move to different parts of the room to give different people attention.
- Occasionally, move close to people, but don't stand too close for too long.
- When you want to make a really important point, stop moving.
- Your movement should not include foot tapping or any other nervous, jerky movement.
- Mix it up.

Part of the value of movement is that you are gently but forcefully coercing your audience into moving their heads and eyes to follow you. If they are moving, they are less likely to fall asleep. Additionally, you are putting your audience on notice, politely, that you might be close to them at any time. This means they had better think twice about checking their e-mail. Conversely, if you stay behind the lectern, audience members feel it is safe for them to read e-mail, doodle, or even chat with people next to them.

The Secret

By walking around the room and getting closer to people, you make yourself a much bigger presence in the room and therefore harder to ignore.

It's not the end of the world to speak from behind a lectern or to stand in one spot, but if you can do something that you already do every day—walk and talk at the same time—and give your audience a much more interesting and dynamic presentation, why not do it?

TJ TV: Joel Osteen doesn't stand behind a lectern. Why should you? Go to www.tjwalker. com, register if you're a first-time visitor, and enter the words OSTEEN LECTERN in the TJ TV form.

TROUBLESHOOTING AND ADAPTING

Should I give my audience fair warning if I know that I have to cover some boring content?

Don't do it! It doesn't work.

Imagine you are going on a date. How impressive would it be if at the beginning of the evening your date said, "I'm sorry, but this is going to be a really lousy date because I'm not good at this sort of thing, and I didn't get enough sleep last night, and my mom picked out this ugly shirt for me to wear." Would that have made the date go better, or would it have just soured things from the start?

Yet I routinely see entrepreneurs, businesspeople, and political candidates start off their presentations by saying things like,

"Sorry, but I know my presentation is really boring!"

"I'd like to apologize for some of my slides being out of order."

"Let me get through this tedious stuff and then we can have fun with your questions."

"I know some of you won't be able to see my slides but . . ."

"I'm pretty nervous about speaking in front of you today."

"I missed my plane and flew all night so I am really tired . . ."

These are *awful* ways to start a presentation. What you are really telling your audience is that you hold them in such low regard that you didn't adequately prepare for them. You are disrespecting them, giving them permission to respond in kind by ignoring you. Is this any way to start a new relationship?

The reality is that you aren't going to help yourself by making excuses or trying to minimize audience expectations. But here is the more important reality: Your audience already has very low expectations for you and every other speaker. Why? Because most presenters are really boring and tedious. Most presenters waste the time of the people they are presenting to. A fairly high percentage of presenters start by making lame excuses or trying to minimize expectations. You, on the other hand, can really distinguish yourself by being interesting and great from the moment you start presenting.

The Secret

You can surpass the expectations of your audience every time you speak not by lowering their expectations, but by exceeding the already low expectations that other presenters have created before you.

Audience members are typically rooting for you, the presenter. They want you to do well. They have a mutual interest in the presentation going well because if it's awful, you will both suffer. If they really didn't want you to do well, they would have figured out some way to avoid being in the room with you. And it's likely that their expectations have been set low. As a result, most business audiences are pleased if you just don't bore them to death. The one big exception is for comedians who have to present in front of a paying audience that is expecting a huge belly laugh every ten seconds. That is the hardest audience to please.

Take this reality, then, and accept it. Use it to your advantage to give you confidence and to set you straight from the very beginning of your presentation. Although you don't want to openly articulate this, everything you communicate with your words, energy, enthusiasm, and body language should say, "This presentation is going to be freakin' fantastic, for you and for me!"

TJ TV: Rudy Giuliani exudes confidence during his speeches, a model we can all try to emulate. To see a Giuliani video clip, go to www.tjwalker.com, register if you're a first-time visitor, and enter the words CONFIDENT SPEAKER in the TJ TV form.

What do I do if I make a mistake or forget what I am about to say?

Don't tell anyone! Don't show anyone!

It really does come down to following these two principles.

Everyone makes mistakes when they present. We forget a point, present something out of order, and talk about a slide that is two slides away instead of the one our audience is looking at. Everyone makes mistakes. But not everyone reacts to their mistakes the same way.

The average presenter will literally say "I'm sorry" to the audience, with a look of extreme sheepishness. When you combine this blunder with the probability that the average speaker is unemotional, bland, and boring through the rest of the speech, the end result is that the only emotional moment in the whole presentation is when the presenter looked and sounded embarrassed.

This moment now stands out as the most interesting and therefore the most memorable. Disaster!

The Secret

Typically, audience members don't notice a presenter's mistakes—until the presenter brings a mistake to the audience's attention by mentioning it.

The foolproof presenter, being human, doesn't aspire to flawless perfection when delivering presentations. But he or she does have one trick up the sleeve that other presenters don't have, and that is the knowledge that if you don't tell your audience you made a mistake, they will likely never figure it out.

Let's look at a few common mistakes and the best way to handle them.

Let's say you deliver a point in your presentation out of order. Well, "order" is a concept in your brain or on your notes. The audience doesn't see that order. They don't have your notes or speech text in front of them. They are just listening to you and trying to understand what you are talking about. So, if you realize you've gone out of order, just go back to the point or points you missed after you finish the current point. Do not tell the audience that this is what you are doing. They don't care.

Every so often, I will start talking about a concept and a story that is supported by a video clip or an image that is two slides away. In that case, when I advance the slide, the wrong slide will come up. But I never panic and I never comment on it. I just calmly advance the Power-Point to the slide that I need. Then I go in reverse when I am ready to go back to the missed point. Thereafter, I have to advance twice to get back to the right place. Guess what? No one ever notices this blunder when I quiz them on it immediately after the presentation. This is because I never show distress. I never utter apologies. I never show concern. I just keep going, and the whole mistake becomes so unmemorable that it is forgotten moments later. Or the audience may even think that I did it on purpose to better meet their needs.

Let's say you are in the middle of making a point and suddenly your brain freezes and you can't remember what to say next. The average presenter will have a look of horror shoot across his face, turn bright red, grimace, apologize to the audience, and then mutter something about having a so called senior moment. But here is what you do if you are a foolproof presenter:

Stop. Look at one person in the audience with an expression on your face that communicates that you just said something so brilliant, she should take a moment to think about it. Next, perhaps ask a question of one person or the whole audience to see if they are with you so far. Or just quietly walk across the room as if to signify a planned, natural transition. Inwardly you are thinking, "Oh no, I forgot what I was supposed to say! What comes next?" But outwardly you are projecting serenity, calm, purposefulness, and a focus on your audience.

Trust me; this technique will work for you the vast majority of the time. Obviously, if you say something so glaringly, factually wrong that everyone will notice (for instance, "the Moon is only nine thousand miles away from the Earth"), then you should instantly and immediately correct yourself, but without unnecessary self-flagellation.

So, if you make a mistake, don't panic. You now have the skills to minimize the damage in the eyes of your audience. And if you master the skill of ignoring your weak moments, you will condition your audience to do the same.

TJ TV: Want more great tips for how to handle mistakes? Go to www.tjwalker.com, register if you're a first-time visitor, and enter the words HANDLE MISTAKES in the TJ TV form.

If my allotted time is cut, what should I eliminate from my presentation?

This is a common situation. You've been told you have thirty minutes to make your presentation to the board on what your department has been doing for the last quarter and why you deserve continued funding. But at the last minute, the organizer whispers in your ear: "We're running behind schedule. You've got fifteen minutes."

Egads!

What do you do now? You have thirty minutes' worth of material. You've rehearsed it, and you've got the time down to exactly thirty minutes. This is unfair! This can't be happening! You played by the rules, why can't everyone else?

Relax. You will get through this.

Here is the first option, and by my estimation, it's what 99 percent of businesspeople do when facing this situation: Comment at the beginning, middle, and end that there is not enough time to cover all of your points, apologizing along the way. Eliminate all of your stories, examples, and case studies to save time. Speak faster than normal to cover all the key points. Sweat. Apologize one last time in your conclusion. And then walk away with an annoyed look on your face.

If you follow this approach, you will be in good company because this is what most people do. However, you won't actually communicate anything, and your presentation will have accomplished nothing. But you don't have to fall into this trap.

Here is what you should do in these situations.

Quickly determine the order of importance of all of your key points and then eliminate the bottom half. (Note that it's always best to know the order of importance of your points so that if you are running long, you can cover those points you think are most important first.)

Never waste even a second of time by talking about the fact that you don't have as much time as you'd like.

Speak at a normal speed in a completely conversational manner, as if you had all the time in the world. If you speak faster, people won't understand you and they'll just think you are nervous, which will make you seem less credible.

WHEN TIME IS CUT, SOMETHING MUST GO. MAKE SURE IT ISN'T YOU.

Deliver every single story, anecdote, and case study you had prepared for the top points you cover.

Never apologize—not even once.

Finish in your allotted time, and act as if this was the best presentation you have ever given and that you are completely satisfied with how it went.

At the conclusion, give people paper or electronic handouts that cover all of the points you had originally planned to discuss.

The Secret

Make the best of every presenting situation. Never complain, never seem nervous or irritated, and never apologize.

It actually can be a blessing to have your time cut moments before you present. It provides a great opportunity for you to demonstrate in front of your boss, colleagues, and clients that you have the ability to adapt quickly, that you can survive under pressure, and that you are flexible and can think on your feet. Too many salespeople, account managers, and executives get put into this situation and all they can do is feel sorry for themselves and make excuses. It's never pretty.

The foolproof presenter realizes there is never an ideal environment for speaking. There will always be distractions—noise from next door, poor lighting, or noisy people in the back of the room. You have to simply size up the opportunity, given what is available in terms of time and resources, and then make the best of it—every time.

TJ TV: Make the most of your time on stage. Go to www.tjwalker.com, register if you're a first-time visitor, and enter the words STAGE TIME in the TJ TV form.

What if I can't answer a question during or after my presentation?

t's nerve-racking when someone, especially a boss or an important client or prospect, asks you a question and you can't answer it. I sympathize with you; really, I do. But this is not an uncommon problem, and the solution is quite simple. So don't panic.

In fact, every time I speak to a large audience of one hundred or more, I ask the following question, "How many of you remember a time when you saw a presenter who couldn't answer a question and he or she was obviously embarrassed?" Sure enough, about 20 percent of the hands go up. This is indeed a real and legitimate concern, but this response is also key to understanding the secret of dealing with the problem.

The Secret

It's not important that you have a full, complete, fascinating answer to every question. What most audiences remember is your reaction to the question, not your answer.

Quite often, when a presenter is asked a tough question, this is what the audience sees:

An expression of "Oh, crap!"

A quick, nervous look up to the heavens, as if waiting for divine intervention.

Beads of sweat breaking out on the presenter's forehead.

The presenter muttering something like "Ugh, this is such a tough question . . . I wish you hadn't asked me that . . ."

The presenter breaking out in nervous laughter.

The presenter slumping and sighing, as if to convey: "You got me! I am a fraud! We all know that I am supposed to know the answer to this question. I stand exposed. I am so ashamed! Please let me go home now and I promise to never bother you again!"

The presenter looking back at the questioner with a barely concealed look of contempt.

It is these emotional and physical reactions that become so memorable to audience members. The real trick, therefore, is not as difficult as having a brilliant answer to every question. The solution is just to not look or sound embarrassed in any way when someone asks you a tough question.

There is no one perfect answer or dodge to tough questions, but here are a few possibilities:

"I know that Jim Smithers in our organization has the complete answer to that question. I will find out from him and e-mail you the answer by 4:00 PM today." The trick is to look comfortable and confident the whole time you are speaking. Don't look evasive. And then actually get back to the person with an answer by four o'clock, as promised.

"I don't know. What I can tell you in general is that . . ." and then bridge to something you do know that touches on the subject of the question. Don't be afraid to say you don't know, but always bridge to something else so that you are not saying *only* "I don't know."

"That's an interesting perspective. Thanks for sharing." This works well if the person asking the question was incredibly long-winded, seemed to give a mini-speech, and was a little wacky. This works well for politicians who get crazy questions at town hall meetings.

You can come up with your own answer, and it will work as long as you seem completely comfortable, relaxed, confident, and not bothered. Remember, there can be no "gotcha" moments in your presentation if you don't act "gotten."

Now that you know how to answer tough questions during your presentation, you can get back to more serious business, like making sure you have an interesting and memorable message for your audience.

TJ TV: Get advice for how to respond when you don't know the answer to a tough question during a presentation. Go to www .tjwalker.com, register if you're a first-time visitor, and enter the words DEER HEADLIGHTS in the TJ TV form.

How do I get rid of my "ums" and "uhs"?

Everyone says the occasional "um" and "uh." Don't beat yourself up if you do. Bill O'Reilly and Martha Stewart both say um and uh all the time, and they both make tens of millions of dollars a year just by speaking! So, let's put your problem in perspective. Bill and Martha are still successful because they have messages that audiences find interesting. Your biggest problem is always making sure you have something interesting to say, not whether you have too many ums and uhs.

However, all things considered, the fewer ums and uhs you have cluttering your speech, the better. The first thing you have to do is actually determine if you have the problem. In my experience, executives and salespeople who think they have a problem with too many ums and uhs rarely do. Those who think they don't have a problem are the ones who often do.

There is only one way to find out. That's right, let's go to the videotape (or audiotape). Record yourself and then note how often you say um, uh, like, or any other annoying filler words. The video will not lie to you. Keep a tally as you watch it.

Although the occasional um or uh isn't the end of the world, you do want to pay especially close attention to how many come out of your mouth in the first thirty seconds of your presentation. This is when you are making your first impression. Sadly, the audience will interpret your ums and uhs to mean that you are scared, nervous, and possibly unprepared. It's okay, of course, to be nervous, but we don't want to let our audience know that.

Saying um or uh is the equivalent of filling up your pauses with punctuation; these sounds are like extra commas. Imagine someone has sent you a cover letter and a resume. Imagine the resume is perfect, but the cover letter has a comma after every word in the first sentence. You could still read the letter, and you could still understand it, but the extra commas would be both annoying and seriously distracting. That is the problem with too many ums and uhs.

How do you get rid of these audible fillers? You should not have someone stand in the back of the room and ring a bell every time you say an um or an uh. That will only make

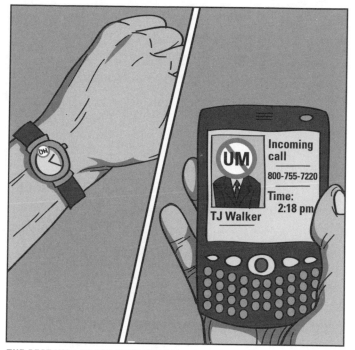

THE BEST WAY TO END YOUR VERBAL TIC IS WITH A LITTLE REMINDER FROM TJ.

you more nervous. You need to recondition your brain. No, you do *not* have to hook up your brain to receive a painful electric shock (this has been suggested to me many times!). I give my clients stickers with the word "um" or "uh" in small type inside a red universal "no" symbol (a circle with a slash through it). I place this sticker on my clients' watches, cell phones, computer monitors, or any-place else where they will see it frequently.

Try it. You look at your watch or cell phone dozens of times a day, and now you get a visual reminder not to say um or uh. After one day, you will still say it, but you will at least be aware of it. After a couple of days, just as you are about to form that sound, the image of "don't say it" pops into your mind. You almost catch it . . . but it still comes out. Drat! But after one week, the image will pop up in your mind and you will be able to hold in the filler word. Now you can simply pause, and this will make you sound more comfortable, confident, and authoritative.

The Secret
Put this image everywhere:

I'm happy to send you some free stickers if you send an e-mail to freestickers@tjwalker.com, or you can just create them yourself. Within one week, your audible fillers problem will no longer be a problem.

The goal is not to have zero verbal tics, so don't beat yourself up or wince in the middle of a presentation if one slips out. The solution I've outlined may sound simple, but it really does work—just not instantly. I've used this technique on billionaire fund managers and politicians around the globe and it works for them—it can work for you too.

TJ TV: Want to see these instructions in a video? Go to www.tjwalker.com, register if you're a first-time visitor, and enter the words TIC BUSTER in the TJ TV form.

Don't I need to speak in a deeper or more authoritative voice to sound serious and credible?

No, you don't need a deeper voice or a different voice from your natural speaking voice.

Most people hate the sound of their own voice. If you record your presentation rehearsal and then watch or listen to it, chances are you won't like yours either. As you may know, how you hear your own voice is not how you actually sound. We hear our own voices distorted through the bones in our skulls from both inside and outside. But when you listen to a recording of your voice, you're hearing the non-distorted version—what everyone else hears when you speak. Your voice sounds very different to you, though, and this is disorienting. This may lead you to the conclusion that you have a strange voice which you should try to change when you are presenting.

Not so fast!

Chances are your voice is fine; it's just different from what you are used to. Different isn't bad; it's just different. In theory, it is possible to have a voice so awful, shrill, and annoying that it seriously detracts from the communication process. But in twenty-five years of training and working with tens of thousands of people around the globe, I have never encountered anyone whose voice was that bad. In fact, I have rarely worked with anyone whose voice is even as bad as Barbara Walters's voice—and she makes tens of millions of dollars a year with her voice!

The Secret
Learn to love the sound of your own voice. If you do, others will follow.

The solution for most people is to simply get used to their voice by hearing it more. Often, women and men feel they need to speak in a lower, deeper voice because they believe this will make them more authoritative and believable. This is very dangerous. Most audiences are very good at detecting someone who is acting phony or trying to put on airs. If you try to sound like you have a rich, full, deep voice and you don't, you'll end up a joke— so don't try it.

If you speak in a monotone (the most common problem that most people associate with their voices), you can easily correct this. Pretend you are talking to five friends at a noisy restaurant. Imagine a crowded bar and waiters in the corner singing "Happy Birthday." If you were telling a story to friends, you would speak louder than normal, with more energy, and with greater variation. That's how you should speak when giving a presentation.

I have studied reports by various clinical researchers who purport to have proof that audiences respond better to deeper voices. I don't buy it. Look at the most successful news anchors and talk show hosts. They don't all sound the same, but they tend to have very full ranges. They hit highs and lows without fear of sounding less authoritative.

There are voice coaches out there who can help anyone improve the quality of his or her voice. If you really feel you need help in this area, you could work with one. But I don't think this is a useful or productive way for most presenters to spend their limited training time. Instead, I would urge you to use your time creating interesting ideas, messages, and stories for your audience and then rehearsing in front of a video camera. This will score you more points than sounding like the guy who does the voice-over for the lottery commercials.

Very few people have a voice so great that they could make a living as a professional voice-over artist. But that's okay, since you probably don't want to be a voice-over artist. But I'm sure that you can use your voice effectively when presenting, as long as you can be heard and understood.

TJ TV: Understand why hating your voice is common and what you can do to improve your voice. Go to www.tjwalker.com, register if you're a first-time visitor, and enter the words VOICE ADVICE in the TJ TV form.

DEVELOPING A LIFETIME PRESENTATION IMPROVEMENT PLAN

What is the single biggest difference between great speakers and average speakers?

I t all comes down to one thing: stories. Great presenters tell interesting, relevant stories to support their message points and make them more memorable; boring speakers make abstract points with lots of facts and numbers. It doesn't matter if you are a motivational speaker or a chemistry teacher, a preacher or a physics professor; this is one of the few universal truths among presenters.

True, you might not look foolish or embarrass yourself if you stick to facts and figures, but you won't actually communicate a message that is remembered or acted upon. On the other hand, I have seen presenters break every single rule of speaking mechanics and still offer a message that really resonated with their audiences because of the interesting, relevant stories they told.

The Secret

If you are a presenter who is doing ninety-nine technical things well— good eye contact, neat appearance, great hand motions—but you fail to tell stories, you will quickly be forgotten by your audience.

Being a great presenter isn't necessarily about putting in the most hours of rehearsal time (though that can help sometimes). It isn't about having a smooth voice or the most expensive suit. Some so-called speaking experts will try to convince you that you need to rehearse one hour for every minute of your speech. Others will want you to practice with marbles in your mouth. Some will want you to record your speech, transcribe it, and then rerecord it until you have eliminated every unnecessary word. These are all irrelevant regarding whether your audience sees you as a great presenter or a mediocre or lousy presenter.

Great speakers are great story gatherers and story retellers. They aren't necessarily more creative or more original or better speechwriters. If you truly want to prepare yourself to be a great speaker and you could ask yourself just one question before each presentation, it should be this: "Do I have an interesting and relevant story for each point of my presentation?" If the answer is yes, then you are ready to be great. If the answer is no, then you are prepared for mediocrity.

TJ TV: Examining the secrets of Howard Stern's success can help you become a better presenter. Go to www.tjwalker.com, register if you're a first-time visitor, and enter the words HOWARD STERN in the TJ TV form.

What role does attitude play in my presentation?

Attitude plays a much bigger role in presentation success than it does in other areas of life. For example, I can go out on a golf course brimming with confidence. I can tell my partners: "I'm going to hit a hole in one. I'm going to make Tiger Woods look like a duffer." And the results will be predictable: I will still shoot 180 (and that's with a mulligan on each hole).

The self-help movement and personal development fields are full of gurus who will tell you attitude is everything. But I would say that in many areas of life, this is bunk. With sports, genetics may play a bigger role. With talents like singing, the ability to be truly great is distributed to a random few. Attitude may not make you great in either field. Fortunately, presenting skills are NOT like that.

Anyone can learn to be an excellent presenter. Your attitude really does have a huge impact on your presentation and on your audience. The sheer act of you looking and sounding like you think you are a great speaker will actually have the effect of making some people believe you are, in fact, an excellent speaker. Because if you believe that you will deliver a great presentation, then you will be confident, and that will go a long way toward making your presentation great in your audience's eyes.

IF YOU SEE YOURSELF AS A SUPERHERO, SO WILL YOUR AUDIENCE.

There are a lot of different styles among world-class speakers, but they all have this one thing in common: They convey through their attitude that they absolutely love speaking, they love the audience they are in front of at that moment, and they are good at what they do. Bill Clinton and Tony Blair make audiences believe that if they weren't being paid fortunes to speak, they'd pay audience members for the right to speak because they are having so much fun.

When Arnold Schwarzenegger speaks to an audience, he doesn't act as if he is filled with self-doubt or nervousness about his accent or his inability to pronounce the word "California." Instead, he exudes a sense of joy and "I can't believe how well this speech is going!" It's contagious.

You can do this too.

The Secret
It is critical that you go into every presentation with the attitude that you are going to nail it, be great, clearly communicate your messages, and accomplish all of your goals.

You must convey this with every part of your body, your voice, your eyes, and your energy. No, you won't be perfect, but audience members are far more likely to pick up on your positive attitude than any minor mistakes or blunders you make.

Unlike learning how to hit a hole in one or dunk a basketball or play concert-level violin, presenting and speaking well are easy skills. When you go into a presentation with a positive and upbeat mental attitude, it's not some phony-baloney, pie-in-the-sky attitude that will set you up for a big fall. Instead, it is an attitude that is positive and realistic at the same time, and it will propel you and your audience toward a successful time together.

TJ TV: Want some video advice on style, substance, and attitude—the three essentials of great speaking? Go to www.tjwalker.com, register if you're a first-time visitor, and enter the words STYLE SUBSTANCE in the TJ TV form.

Who are the best presenters in the world I should emulate?

have my favorites, but you should find your own. Personally, I like watching and listening to Tony Blair, Warren Buffett, Steve Jobs, Oprah Winfrey, Rush Limbaugh, Jim Hightower, Pat Buchanan, Bill Clinton, and recently, Barack Obama. I also enjoy vintage Ronald Reagan and Winston Churchill. But you might hate my taste in presenters—that's okay.

What is important is that you develop your own taste in speakers, just like you do in musicians. You also need to develop the skill of separating content from delivery.

The Secret

If you watch and listen to only people you agree with, you will limit your abilities to improve as a speaker.

If you are a liberal Democrat, I urge you to listen to conservative radio icon Rush Limbaugh for fifteen minutes a week. I'm not asking you to share his beliefs, but you can learn a great deal about communicating by listening to the cleverness with which he packages his messages. If you are a conservative Republican, you could benefit greatly by watching Oprah Winfrey. You might not love her social messages or her Democratic politics, but you will learn from a true master of empathy and audience connection.

At the risk of making your spouse annoyed with you, I urge you to channel surf more. Stop on C-SPAN and watch congressional speeches for three minutes at a time. Analyze what you like and don't like about a presenter's techniques and style. Sure, you can continue to analyze and judge messages, but learn from the speakers' presenting skills as well.

It's not that I want you to watch Governor Schwarzenegger on *Larry King* and start talking with an Austrian accent, but I do want you to make mental notes on your likes and dislikes. You need to be yourself when you are presenting, but each of us is made up of little experiences and preferences, and we can identify them in the people we watch.

Don't limit yourself to your own genre. If you are a banker, don't just watch CNBC; watch Comedy Central to see how great comedians operate. If you are a politician, don't just limit yourself to CNN and C-SPAN; try to watch the great sportscasters on ESPN.

If you continue to watch other successful presenters and look for techniques that you like and don't like, you will improve. In fact, you won't be able to help it. If presenting becomes a passion for you, you will get better at it. The best athletes watch videos of themselves and their competition. You get good at what you focus on. If you focus on great presenters, your own standards will be elevated in the process.

Those who learn to present successfully usually are the most successful in all walks of life. Much has been written about the traits of great leaders, but I would submit that the only consistent trait among world-renowned leaders is that they are effective presenters.

Being a great leader isn't about being tall—look at Ross Perot and Dr. Ruth.

It's not about having great hair—look at Dr. Phil and Donald Trump.

It's not about wearing the right power suit—look at Steve Jobs in his jeans and mock turtleneck.

It's not about getting up early in the morning—Churchill loved sleeping late.

It's not about traditional family values—as thrice-married Rudy Giuliani can tell you.

It's not about belief in God or religion—look at atheists Ted Turner and Albert Einstein.

It's not even about being ethical or law-abiding—as infomercial guru, best-selling author, and twice-convicted felon Kevin Trudeau can tell you.

SUCCESSFUL PRESENTERS TO STUDY

Ronald Reagan

Oprah Winfrey

Steve Jobs

YOU!

THERE IS SOMETHING TO LEARN FROM ALL SUCCESSFUL PRESENTERS ... INCLUDING YOURSELF!

Every one of the people I just mentioned is a leader to millions, yet each of them breaks someone's definition of a leader. I'm not saying these are good trends, just reality. But they do all have one thing in common: They are all great at presenting their ideas to others.

But there is really only one great presenter that you need to watch regularly and repeatedly. You. It's not enough to watch others; you must watch yourself. You need to watch yourself regularly, not once every five years—which is just often enough to be horrified by how much you've aged. (It's happening to me too, but it doesn't hurt much because I see myself on video every week). You need to watch yourself every time you make a presentation. It doesn't matter if it's at a PTA meeting or a friend's wedding. Tape yourself and figure out what you do that you think is great—then do more of it. What do you not like? Do less of it. If you don't consider yourself great yet, you will soon if you practice enough and follow the principles covered in this book.

If you do this long enough, what you will find is that when you watch world-famous celebrities on TV speaking, you will no longer be in awe. You will appreciate the things they do well, but you will know exactly what they are doing and why you like it. And you will find fault with even the best. Eventually, you will conclude that you can do as well as or better than anyone you see presenting.

So, develop your presenting role models, and make sure that in the long run you are your own ultimate role model.

TJ TV: Paul Harvey is a great role model for developing presentation skills. To watch a video analysis of Paul Harvey, go to www.tjwalker.com, register if you're a first-time visitor, and enter the words PAUL HARVEY in the TJ TV form.

Isn't being a truly great presenter a talent you have to be born with?

No.

Anyone can be a great presenter. Presenting well is not a rare talent, like playing concert-level piano or shooting six under par on a world-class golf course. Presenting well is a skill that anyone can learn with a little focus. It's more like making tasty Toll House chocolate chip cookies: If you follow the recipe and pay attention, you will create a satisfying final product.

You already know how to talk, to engage others, and to be understood. For most people, then, learning how to be a great presenter doesn't require learning a new skill set. It just requires an understanding of how to transfer a skill set they already have to a different setting.

The Secret

If you have ever had a single interesting conversation with one other person, then you already have all of the technical skills you need to be an excellent presenter.

Most people let fear and nervousness psych them out of delivering a good presentation. Once they learn how to control their nerves, the speaking comes naturally. All they have to do is throw in a little organization and specific message points into their natural speaking talent, and they're set.

I see average executives and salespeople transform themselves into great presenters every day. But don't take my word for it. Just look at some of the most well-known and highly regarded speakers in history.

Dr. Martin Luther King, Jr., earned a "C" in public speaking class while in college.

President John F. Kennedy was such a nervous speaker that people who sat behind him saw his legs shake while he spoke.

Conservative radio talk show host Rush Limbaugh barely passed his college public speaking course.

Rev. Jesse Jackson had a horrible stutter as a child.

Vice President Joe Biden had a horrible stutter well into his college years, yet he spoke his way into the U.S. Senate at age 29!

Excellent presenters are not born, they are made.

People don't grow up practicing their presenting skills. People don't get coached daily for years on their presenting skills. The reality is that most presenters are awful, untrained, unrehearsed, boring, and ordinary because they don't practice and they have never been coached. But it is crucial for you to realize that you already have all the talents and abilities you need. Not to be a competent presenter, an okay presenter, or an above-average presenter, however. You have everything you need to be a *great*, *foolproof* presenter.

TJ TV: Martin Luther King, Jr., wasn't born a great speaker. Go to www.tjwalker.com, register if you're a first-time visitor, and enter the words **BORN GREAT** in the TJ TV form.

Acknowledgments

I'd like to thank the many people who have listened to me speak since my first presentation at the 1975 Bruns Avenue Elementary School graduation ceremony. Special thanks go to my mother, Patti, who was at the first speech and continues to be a constant source of help and comfort for me and the team here at Media Training Worldwide.

This book is the result of a collaboration I have had with two main groups: the thousands of executives I have trained during the last two decades and the small team of professionals I work with here at Media Training Worldwide, including Kris Gentile, Jess Todtfeld, Mike Bako, and Jennifer Wallerstein.

My colleague and coauthor, Jess Todtfeld, is a constant source of speaking expertise, inspiration, and good humor.

While I freely acknowledge that I still might not be the best speaker in the world, I take a back seat to no one when it comes to my interest and passion for watching great speakers and learning how they do what they do. I'd like to acknowledge my appreciation and debt to all of the great speakers of the twentieth and twenty-first centuries. I may have only seen you on TV, but your words inspired me nonetheless.

Special thanks need to go to my friends and colleagues who stood by me during my lean years. While my many clients pay me handsomely these days, there were many years when I spoke without a business model and had to live off of the basement couches of friends who stood by me through bad times and good. They include Rich Gladstone, Joe McHugh, Bob Bowdon, and Stan Adkins.

Since I am a color-blind speaker with little sense of aesthetics, credit for the great look and feel of this book belongs to the excellent team at Greenleaf Book Group. Thanks for making this whole project the perfect blend of passion and professionalism.

Finally, thanks to everyone who ever had the nerve to get up and speak in front of other people. Without you, I'd be out of a job.

—TJ Walker

As TJ's humble colleague and president of his company, I want to thank him for including me in the exciting ride that is TJWalker Speaking, The Speaking Channel, Media Training Worldwide, and projects yet to be hatched. He has been an inspiring mentor. Now, the secrets I've acquired about speaking are available for the masses! Apply the strategies behind these secrets; they work! I use them every time I speak, whether it's a speech, a networking event, or a phone call.

Additional thanks go to my parents, Ellen Glass and Stewart Todtfeld, both educators, for bringing me into this world and for encouraging and influencing me in tremendous ways. Other VIPs worthy of mention include Guy Kawasaki, Robert Kiyosaki, Rick Frishman, Karrah Kaplan, Shannon Koenig, Brian Kilmeade, Steve Doocy, Mike Straka, Jordan Chariton, Steve & Bill Harrison, Jackie Soares, and Alan Klein. I'd like to give a special shout-out to Tye Farrell, long-time friend and entrepreneurial comrade, whose creative know-how has helped me a great deal.

Both TJ and I would like to give special thanks to JoAnne, my wife, for her publishing and editorial expertise on this book. And her unyielding love and support for me have enabled me to focus much of my energies on my dreams.

And to everyone who picks up this book, reads it, and reaps the benefits, I have only two things to say to you: "Bravo!" and "You're welcome!" —**Jess Todtfeld**

About the Authors

TJ Walker is the CEO of TJWalker Speaking, Inc., and the founder of Media Training Worldwide. In addition, he educates people on speaking, presenting, and working with the media through a variety of efforts.

- Keynote speaker—TJ gives more than one hundred keynote speeches and training sessions each year on leadership, communication, media, and presentation skills. His most popular speech is "Bully Pulpits: Speaking Secrets of World Famous Leaders."

- Television host and producer—TJ is the host of two daily television shows on The Speaking Channel (www.speakingchannel.tv). *Bully Pulpits: Speaking Secrets of World Famous Leaders* features short video clips of everyone from Franklin Roosevelt to Ronald Reagan. *Speaking with TJ Walker* gives practical, nuts-and-bolts advice on all aspects of speaking and dealing with the media.

- Online training TJWalker Speaking Online (tjwalker.com) features 28 interactive online presentation training courses.

- Author—TJ is the author of *TJ Walker's Secret to Foolproof Presentations*, *Media Training A-Z*, *Presentation Training A-Z* and more than one hundred other books, videos, DVDs, CDs, software programs, and other learning tools.
- Commentator—A frequent news commentator, TJ has hosted more than two thousand talk radio and television shows and has been featured numerous times on such networks as CNN, Headline News, ABC-TV, Fox News Channel, MSNBC, Court TV, Bloomberg TV, Comedy Central, National Public Radio, ABC Radio, NBC Radio, CBS Radio, and Westwood One.

TJ's customers include Qualcomm, Microsoft, HP, Bank of America, Unilever, Allstate, Miss Universe Organization, EMC, The Hartford, Dun and Bradstreet, US Trust, and hundreds more. TJ has worked personally with prime ministers, Nobel Peace Prize winners, beauty queens, CEOs, professional athletes, and members of Congress.

TJ was a Merit Scholar at Duke University where he graduated magna cum laude. He has lectured or trained at Yale University, Columbia University, and Princeton University.

Connect with TJ on Facebook, Linkedin, Twitter (tjwalker), through his blog (tjwalker.com/blog), via email (tj@tjwalker.com), or by phone (877-TJ-Walker, 212-764-4955).

Jess Todtfeld is president of Media Training Worldwide, which has offices in India, Korea, the Middle East, Romania, and Portugal. One of the leading speaking and media training authorities in the United States, he gives customizable keynote speeches nationwide on topics related to communication and speaking skills.

In 2003, Jess founded Success in Media, Inc., a full-service speaker training firm. Media Training Worldwide acquired the firm in August 2007.

Jess brings with him twelve-plus years of experience as a television producer on the national level for networks including NBC, ABC, and FOX. During that time he booked and produced more than 4,000 segments. Ten of those twelve years were at Cable TV's #1 news channel, FOX News Channel; two years with cable's #1 prime time show, *The O'Reilly Factor*; and seven years with cable's #1 morning show, *FOX & Friends*.

With more than fifteen years of experience, Jess trains CEOs, experts, authors, and spokespeople in two ways: (1) To better *leverage* every media appearance, and (2) to give presentations and speeches that are more *memorable* and create more *action*. Since 2007, he has also hosted the Speaking Channel, an online TV show devoted to news and information related to communication and speaking skills.

Todtfeld has trained clients from IBM, AIG, AARP, USAToday.com, the World Children's Wellness Foundation, Edelman Public Relations, Ruder Finn Public Relations, Fine Living Network, North Face apparel, and the ASPCA. He has also been featured in *Promote Like a Pro*, *The Weekend Entrepreneur*, and *Author 101: Bestselling Book Publicity*.